"No matter if you're wondering if you can write or if you have pages of publications behind you, there is something in this book for you. There are slivers of truth in everyday events that are enriching both from developing your craft and from the point of view of experiencing life intensely. This would be an excellent book to pick up if you're blocked, and even better if you are at your peak production. So few books make instruction interesting, but this succeeds in doing just that."

—D-L Nelson, author of *The Card* and *Chickpea Lover: Not a Cookbook*

"Whether you want to write essays, short stories, prose poems, or memoirs, you will find a kaleidoscope of practical hints and wisdom in Susan Tiberghien's book which will inspire your imagination."

—Maureen Murdock, author of *Unreliable Truth: On Memoir and Memory*

"Reading *One Year to a Writing Life* I hear Susan's voice and relive the nurturing experience of her workshops, that was so important for my way as a writer. This book is her workshops, to revisit again and again."

—Sylvia Petter, author of *The Past Present* and *Back Burning*

"If I had to choose one writing book to have on my shelves, it would be Susan Tiberghien's *One Year to a Writing Life*. It is a treasure chest of jewels—elegant quotes from some of our greatest writers, a myriad of stunning writing samples, and imaginative exercises to help you hone your skills and tone your writing muscles. No matter what you're writing or where you are on the creative path, this book will feel like it's meant for you."

—Jan Phillips, author of *The Art of Original Thinking, Marry YourMuse,*
Divining the Body and *God Is at Eye Level*

"Susan Tiberghien is an artist of the word, the thought, the soul. *One Year to a Writing Life* skillfully explores the nuts and bolts of the craft hand in hand with the intangibles of fantasy in the same way a Buddhist monk might blend scrubbing a temple floor with spiritual enlightenment. Amidst a collage of the collective wisdom of writers from many generations and cultures, she provides a series of practical exercises that allow the user to chart his or her own way. Her twelve lessons are structured enough to organize twelve month's hard work, yet so flexible you can view them as the twelve strikes of a human clock, as the ingredients to an alchemist's potion that will open up a writer's unique perspective, an existence she best describes from her own experience: 'the colors were brighter, the sounds deeper.'"

—M.M. Tawfik, author of *A Naughty Boy Called Antar*

"Under the care of Susan Tiberghien's inspired instruction, a fledgling author can learn to write clear, centered, original work assured of praxis built on rock."

—Jan Kemp, poet

"This book, because of Tiberghien's deep life experience, will give you courage, keep you company, and lead you to the flame burning in any creative act."

—Wallis Wilde-Menozzi, author of *Mother Tongue: An American Life in Italy*

About the Author

Susan M. Tiberghien is the American-born author of three books, *Looking for Gold, Circling to the Center, and Footsteps: A European Album.* She has been published widely in journals and anthologies. Tiberghien teaches and lectures at graduate programs, at C.G. Jung Centers, and at writers' conferences in the United States and in Europe. She lives with her family in Geneva, Switzerland, where she directs the Geneva Writers' Group that she founded in 1993.

One Year to a Writing Life

One Year to a Writing Life

Twelve Lessons to Deepen Every Writer's Art and Craft

SUSAN M. TIBERGHIEN

Marlowe & Company
New York

One Year to a Writing Life:
Twelve Lessons to Deepen Every Writer's Art and Craft

Copyright © 2007 Susan M. Tiberghien

Published by
Marlowe & Company
An Imprint of Avalon Publishing Group, Incorporated
245 West 17th Street • 11th Floor
New York, NY 10011-5300

AVALON
publishing group incorporated

Library of Congress Cataloging-in-Publication Data

Tiberghien, Susan M.
  One year to a writing life : twelve lessons to deepen every writer's art and craft /
Susan Tiberghien.
    p. cm.
  Includes bibliographical references.
  ISBN-13: 978-1-60094-058-3
  ISBN-10: 1-60094-058-7
  1. Authorship. I. Title.
PN147.T53 2007
808'.02--dc22

                              2007014387

              9 8 7 6 5 4 3 2 1

              Designed by Maria E. Torres
              Printed in the United States of America

To the writers who come to my workshops,
to the writers who open this book

Everything is gestation and then bringing forth. To let each impression and each germ of a feeling come to completion wholly in itself, in the dark, in the inexpressible, the unconscious, beyond the reach of one's intelligence, and await with deep humility and patience the birth-hour of a new clarity: that alone is living the artist's life: in understanding as in creating.

—Rainer Maria Rilke

Contents

Acknowledgments

I wish to thank the following people who made this book possible: Pierre-Yves Tiberghien, my husband, and our children; Eunice and Hollister Marquardt, my parents; Ann Boehm, my sister; Amy Clampitt, Robert Russell, Wallis Wilde-Menozzi, my writing friends

From the first workshops: Sally Alderson, Mary Guerry, Sandi Stromberg, Kristina Schellinski, Mavis Guinard, Dianne Dicks

From the International Women's Writing Guild: Hannelore Hahn, D.H. Melhem, Pat Carr, Susan Baugh, Maureen Murdock, Myra Shapiro, Eunice Scarfe, Lynne Barrett, Carol Peck

From the Geneva Writers' Group: Karen McDermott, Alistair Scott, Jo Ann Rasch, Sylvia Petter, D-L Nelson, Kathleen Walsh, Eliza Wangerin, Lang-Hoan Pham, Grace Yagtug

From C.G. Jung Institutes: Robert Hinshaw, Bernard Sartorius, Christina Ekeus-Oldfelt, Margaret Speicher, Blanche Gray, April Barrett, Janet Careswell

From the Paris Writers' Workshop: Ellen Hinsey, Rose Burke, Denis Hirson, David Applefield

From the Hudson Valley Writers' Center: Dare Thompson

From the Geneva Writers' Conferences: Thomas E. Kennedy, Stephen Belber, Lee Gutkind, Larry Habegger, Isabel Huggan, Michael Steinberg, Peter and Jeanne Meinke

With special appreciation to
Susan Schulman, my agent, who believes in this book
Renée Sedliar, my editor, who knows this book by heart
You both are gifts in my writing life.

Introduction

Ask writers to define the writing life and you will get many answers. Annie Dillard says that it is "life at its most free." Julia Cameron says "the writing life is a simple life." For Stephen King, it's "a brighter, more pleasant place." From William Strunk, Jr. to Brenda Ueland to John Gardner, writers have been offering counsel to encourage people to write. And all the words come back to one fundamental truth: a writing life is a creative life. This book invites you to enter the way of writing. If you are well along the way, it will be a companion, offering both inspiration and instruction.

For me it has become a life that awakens to birdsong in early morning, that lingers with sunlight in late afternoon. For me it is a life that slows down to touch each moment, a life that deepens from an inner source. I was fifty years old when I started along the way. I had been writing letters, various papers, and journal entries, but not thinking of myself as a writer. In fact, because I was living in another language, I thought my creative writing had run into a dead end. My life was full—French husband, six French-speaking children, French in-laws and friends, part-time teaching in France (and Belgium, Italy, and Switzerland)—yet I longed for something more. Once I acknowledged that I wanted to be a writer, the well within me filled with fresh creativity. Returning to English, I started to note my dreams, to write regularly, and to craft stories.

For my fiftieth birthday, I went to my first writing workshop, where I met the celebrated poet Amy Clampitt. At age sixty, she was teaching for the first time. We became fast friends, two cronies sharing our wonder at a patch of zinnias, a kingfisher taking flight. She gave me faith in my words. I started publishing short stories and narrative essays in reviews and journals, and I started living as a writer. The colors were brighter, the sounds deeper.

I went from flashes to lengthier narratives, stretching and expanding my writing to a book about dreams, one about silent prayer, and another about crossing cultures. As I entered the writing life, it entered me. I found it natural to share this life, and so I started teaching workshops in Europe and across the United States—at writers' centers, at the International Women's Writing Guild conferences, at C.G. Jung Institutes, and every month here in Geneva, Switzerland, where I live. Many of the participants of these workshops are now published and many continue to attend, returning each time to immerse themselves in the way of writing.

One Year to a Writing Life presents twelve workshops drawn from over fifteen years of teaching. The lessons dovetail inspiration and instruction. The first component, inspiration, comes from my trust in writing as a way of life: a trust nourished by practice. It is a habit. A person who writes has the habit of writing. The word habit refers to a routine, but also to a stole, to a costume befitting a calling. In the same way that a monk puts on a traditional habit, so the writer puts on a traditional habit. As writers we find where we are comfortable and with a stole over our shoulders, we write.

A writing life springs from the one creative source that is within each of us. It is the same source in all spiritual traditions. For me, the source is God. For others it is Allah, the Tao, the Spirit. When we tap into this source, we become co-creators with our Creator. If the well is blocked, the water does not rise. But if we clear away the clutter, our creativity overflows and touches those around us. Inspiration is breathing. We breathe in, we dip into the well for water. We breathe out, we carry the water with us. We do this with words, finding our stories in the dark and sharing them in the light.

The second component of the lessons, instruction, comes from my trust in writing as a process. I appreciate a well-turned sentence that gives life to an image, a dialogue that shares its secrets, a page of prose that lingers in the mind and sinks into the heart. In examining how this is done, we sharpen our writing skills, clarify our thinking, and deepen our awareness— of ourselves and of the world around us. We work as artists.

Both inspiration and instruction are strengthened through continued reading and reflection. Amy Clampitt was once asked at a writers' conference, "What do writers need most?" She answered, "Predecessors." We enter this world on the shoulders of our predecessors—emerging from centuries of thought, reflection, storytelling, and dreams. We learn by reading others, by reaching down into our universal roots.

It is this combination of inspiration and instruction that under-pins *One Year to a Writing Life*. Each chapter includes examples of writing from over the centuries, though mostly contempo-rary, to show how different authors craft their words and send their voices into the world. You will learn from Plato, St. Augus-tine, Montaigne, Virginia Woolf, Brenda Ueland, Eduardo Galeano, Annie Dillard, Terry Tempest Williams, Orhan Pamuk, and many others. Also included are exercises to guide you to fresh spurts of writing, suggesting ways to strengthen your craft and develop your voice.

One Year to a Writing Life opens its pages to your own rhythm and pleasure. The proposed cycle of twelve lessons is adaptable. You can work alone, reading the lesson in the same way that you would follow a workshop, taking about two hours for each, including the guided exercises. The structure is one lesson per month, but you can spend less time, working more quickly, or more time, going back to the teaching notes and examples, reading the books mentioned in the bibliographies, and devoting more attention to the exercises. While the lessons do build on one another, they can also be read in a different order according to whatever works best for you as you develop your own writing life.

Another way to use this book is to work with others, leading a group of writers or teaching a class in a writers' program, sharing the instruction, examples, and exercises. A writing group is precious. So is a writing friend. Writing is lonely. Some-times you long for the company of other writers, for the energy that comes when writing in a group. If you cannot find a group, create one. Ask a few friends to come to your home and write together, or find one writing friend. Follow the lessons in the book, reading the examples and doing the exercises together.

Then share your work, listening and learning from one another, grateful for the attention.

The year begins with the most natural opening into a writing life: Journal Writing. When you write a little each day (*jour* means day in French), journaling becomes a daily practice. From your journals you will move to Lesson Two, Personal Essays, a flourishing form of nonfiction reflecting each individual voice. Personal essays transition to Lesson Three, Opinion and Travel Essays. From your journals, you can also move to fiction with Lesson Four, Short Stories, and a special focus on the Short-Short.

Lesson Five, Dreams and Writing, brings you to the second stretch and asks you to go more deeply within. Dreams have long been a doorway for many writers. This lesson guides you in writing from your own dreams in order to deepen your creativity. Then follows Lesson Six, Dialogue, a difficult craft but one that, when well done, draws the reader right to the page and into the story. From there, you will weave stories, dreams, and dialogue together with Lesson Seven: Tales: Folk, Fairy, and Contemporary. Lesson Eight, Poetic Prose and the Prose Poem, turns your attention to the elements of poetry, encouraging you to look at rhythm, imagery, and compression in your writing.

The Alchemy of Imagination, Lesson Nine, leads you to the last stretch and still deeper writing through alchemy, an ancient way of refining life's experiences to find the gold within. Mosaics and Memoir, Lesson Ten, brings the different pieces that you've crafted during the year together in a mosaic as a form of memoir. This mosaic pattern may also be used in writing fiction. Lesson Eleven, Rewriting, examines what makes for good writing and guides you in re-visioning what you want to say. Finally, Lesson Twelve, Writing the Way Home, offers writing—in the form that has become yours—as the way to find your center, your true home.

In *Memories, Dreams, Reflections,* C.G. Jung describes a dream he had in his early years: "It was night in some unknown place and I was making slow and painful headway against a mighty wind. Dense fog was flying everywhere. I had my hands cupped around a tiny light which threatened to go out at any moment. Everything depended on my keeping this little light alive." This is the light within each of us, the light that we bring into the world.

One Year to a Writing Life will lead you to this light. With your words, you become a light bearer in the world.

One Year to a Writing Life

Journal Writing

The first step toward a writing life—and its foundation—is journal writing. To write well takes practice. A writer writes, just as a runner runs and a dancer dances. Journal writing is practice and much more. With your words you give life to what you see, what you hear, what you touch. In this way you transform the outer thing that you see or touch into something inner. You bridge the outer and inner worlds, the visible and the invisible. This is the gift of journaling. Your daily life calls you in a thousand directions; journal writing centers you. You slow down and write. You learn to look anew at the world around you.

In my journal, when I write about ordinary gray pebbles at my front door, I see hundreds of them at my feet. They all look pretty much the same—gray, dull, and uneven in shape. But if I pick one up in my hand and write about it, it becomes unique. I see that it is shaped like a house, like the drawings I did as a child. I imagine a door. The pebble is a small world in itself. In writing about it, I touch its mystery. It is the same if I write about an oak tree in the park or my grandson on a swing in a ray of sunlight. My words take me deeper. As Marion Woodman writes, "My journal became a mirror in which I could see and hear my truth resonating in my own daily experience."

INTRODUCTION TO JOURNAL WRITING

My journals are gleanings: what I have gathered from a walk in the Swiss vineyards, the grapes that are left after the harvest, what I have gleaned from a day. The French word for day, *jour,* points the way for a journal: a day's work, a day's discovery, written down. We find the same French root in the word journey, which is defined in the dictionary as a day's travel. So a journal is a day's journey.

I do not necessarily, arbitrarily, write every day in my journal. But I always have it close by, and from one day to the next I often write down what I have gathered along the way. I write about a dream (even a sliver of a dream), the smell of freshly cut grass, a conversation with one of my children, sky turning pink in early evening, a quote from a book. I glean the fruits that I find along the way—including the wrinkled ones that have been discarded, the ones that don't taste very good. And maybe I add a flower, a cinquefoil pressed flat, or a leaf turned gold from the late summer sun. My journal is like my writing desk, filled with notes and souvenirs.

I start my day with quiet time. I go to my desk in my small study and sit in stillness. A silent prayer, a wordless meditation, and then I write. This is my usual time for writing an entry in my journal, but I don't write every morning; sometimes I simply look out the window. Then I try to live my day as a journey.

When a flower opens in sunlight, when a cloud beckons, I write that into my journal.

Brenda Ueland, in her classic *If You Want to Write,* first published in 1938, writes that she kept a slovenly, headlong, helter-skelter diary for years. She wrote in it, off and on, day after day, "and sometimes as minutely and accurately as the Recording Angel." It was not a "had lunch" diary, but rather anything she thought, saw, or felt. And the more impulsive the writing was, the closer it was to the things that interested her. She wrote that this made her appreciate the act of writing. Before, she had found it boring, dreaded, and effortful. Journal writing showed her who she was—what to discard in herself and what to respect and love. With every sentence she wrote she learned something. It did her good. It stretched her understanding. She assures her readers that it will be so for every one of them.

George Plimpton, the late editor of *The Paris Review,* was asked in an interview in the publication *The Country and Abroad* if he had any advice to give to aspiring authors. He said, "Well, yes— keep a journal. The best thing to do if you are going to write is to write." And it is best not to wait around. He said he used to be a tank driver in the military and if he let the tank sit around without using it, it got sort of stodgy and didn't want to move. He needed to exercise the tank all the time to keep it running. That's what a writer should do with his pen. Exercise it. Write with it all the time. Plimpton said that the great regret of his life was that he didn't start keeping a journal from when he was young.

So why journal? Here are some of the reasons.

— To establish the habit of writing (A writer writes.)
— To capture memories (places, characters, conversations, events)

— To discover what you think and feel (each time going deeper)
— To find your voice (When does your writing sound the most natural? Look at your entries to see at what time of day and in what place you write most easily. Track your writing habits.)
— To take risks (in a private place)
— To plant seeds for stories (move from image to story)

Every lesson in this book will include spurts of free-writing. This is how you can let go of your editor self—the one who always interrupts, who tells you that your writing is not good enough. In a later lesson you will work with revising, but for now you let the editor within go somewhere else. In free-writing, you write without stopping, without erasing, without rereading. In *Writing Down the Bones,* Natalie Goldberg insists on timed writings, whether they be ten minutes or a half an hour; just keep your hand moving. Julia Cameron, in *The Artist's Way,* proposes morning pages, three pages of longhand writing, strictly stream-of-consciousness, every morning upon rising before doing anything else, in order to get beyond our internal censors. All you need is some paper or an empty journal, a pen, a place to sit down, and the desire to turn your attention inward.

Stop now and write a journal entry. Start with today, the place, the date, and write a short journal entry—slovenly, head-long, impulsive, honest as Brenda Ueland urged. Write from the moment, what you see and feel, here and now. Write freely. As Peter Elbow suggests in *Writing with Power*, free-write, simply write without stopping. Or flow-write, as Marlene Schiwy suggests in *A Voice of One's Own,* stressing that this way of writing flows from your pen to the paper. Time yourself for ten minutes and write about what you see and feel, at this moment, wherever you are, starting with the place and date.

✎ Exercise: Write a short journal entry. Ten minutes.

When you have finished, give your entry a title. Take a few moments to do this. Naming is important; it gives your work recognition and will make it easier to find an entry again. You may want to highlight your titles.

EXAMPLES OF JOURNAL WRITING

Here are two examples of journal writing to show the literary possibilities inherent in journal entries and the breadth of what you can discover when you journal. The first example is from *A Walk Between Heaven and Earth* by Burghild Nina Holzer. She wrote the book in the form of a journal over the course of a year, using the journal to track her own footprints and help others walk their own paths. Holzer tells us that when we write in a journal, we go for a stroll, without purpose or direction. We start one day and walk for a while, write for a while, and then stop. What we have is a fragment, a record of our awareness. The next day we do it again. And perhaps the next. And the next. Soon we have many fragments—of ourselves, or our awareness of the world. Here is one of Holzer's fragments.

SAN FRANCISCO, NOVEMBER 23, MONDAY, NOON [1987]
This morning I got up at dawn, but when I was all dressed I felt exhausted and very dreamy. So I decided to go back to bed again and sleep. Perhaps I wasn't done dreaming. I

looked out the bedroom window, and a hawk flew by and
settled on the big pine tree, on top of it, and waited for
the sun. The light was just rising, and his head was facing
east. And I stood by the window, and then he turned his
head and looked at me. Then he turned back and waited
for the sun. So I decided to sit down and wait for the
sun also.

Hawks have been everywhere where I am recently, even
here in the city. It is odd and wonderful.

I went back to bed and dreamed it was dawn, and
dreamed I was floating, weightlessly, in coral light.

Sometimes it seems as if one thing has nothing to do
with another thing, but it does. The trick is to write it
down. Not to figure it out. To write it down, one vision at
a time.

To write it down, one vision at a time. To watch the hawk. To
write it down. To follow the image. To let the hawk teach her
to wait for the sun. And then to dream of floating in coral
light.

The second example is from Ettie Hillesum's *An Interrupted
Life,* a journal of her last two years in Amsterdam, and then in
the transit camp at Westerbork before she was deported in one
of the weekly freight cars to the camps in Poland. She met her
death at Auschwitz in 1943 at the age of twenty-nine.

FROM THE ENTRY, SATURDAY MORNING, TEN O'CLOCK
[14 MARCH 1942]

The branches of the tree outside my window have been
lopped off. The night before, the stars had still hung like
glistening fruit in the heavy branches, and now they

climbed, unsure of themselves, up the bare, ravaged trunk. Oh, yes, the stars: for a few nights, some of them, lost, deserted, grazed over the wide, forsaken, heavenly plain.

For a moment, when the branches were being cut, I became sentimental. And for that moment I was deeply sad. Then I suddenly knew: I should love the new landscape too, love it in my own way. Now the two trees rise up outside my window like imposing, emaciated ascetics, thrusting into the bright sky like two daggers.

And on Tuesday evening the war raged once again outside my window and I lay there watching it all from my bed . . .

Hillesum chronicled her day-by-day discovery of her own self in the pages of her journal. Each entry took her to a deeper understanding and to a deeper strength. Here the reader sees her transform her sadness in seeing the branches lopped off into the perception of a new landscape where the trees are menacing daggers thrusting into bright sky. And she will love the new landscape in her own way.

Now read these examples again and look for images that resonate for you. Read slowly and circle the images. In the first example of Holzer's journal, she herself circles the hawk. In the second one by Hillesum, there are the lopped-off branches, the stars hanging like glistening fruit, the ravaged trunk, the trees looking like emaciated ascetics. In this way you train yourself to pay attention to images, to write them down, one at a time. The world around you becomes a wide screen offered each day.

✎ Exercise: Read the two examples slowly and circle or write down a list of the images that resonate. Five minutes.

Next return to the journal entry you wrote earlier, read slowly, and circle the images that call to you, that vibrate. If there are no vibrant images in your journal entry, close your eyes and allow one to emerge. Let it surface on its own. What image appears? If you have circled several images, choose one. Hold it in your imagination. Now describe it in a free-write. Let your image lead you, not your mind. Look again at how Holzer wrote about her hawk teaching her to watch the sunrise. How Hillesum started with lopped off branches and moved to ascetics thrusting into the sky like two daggers.

✎ Exercise: Describe in a free-write an image from your journal. Ten minutes.

DRAWING A MANDALA WITH THE JOURNAL IMAGE

We will be working with mandalas twice during this year. A mandala is the Sanskrit word for circle, the symbol of wholeness, the symbol of the cosmos in its entirety. The first representations of mandalas go back to 30,000 years to Paleolithic times, when they were carved onto rocks in South Africa. Whether a mandala is manifested in a cave drawing or in a star or a rose, its center is one. When you enter this center, you are one with the universe. As you look at a mandala, your eyes are drawn to the center. From there the eyes go outward to the circumference and then return back to the center to one-ness.

This explains why in Tibetan Buddhism the mandala is an object of meditation, leading to an at-oneness with the world. Just so, the rose windows in Gothic cathedrals are designed to uplift the soul to the Divine. And in Native American tradition, mandalas represent the soul's search for wholeness and are used for healing.

Carl Jung discovered mandalas in early midlife as he was working deeply with his dreams. He started sketching circular drawings in his notebook every morning, seeing them as cryptograms of the state of his self. He often drew images in the center of his mandalas—for example, a magnolia blossom from a dream he describes in *Memories, Dreams, Reflections*. In the dream, he found himself in Liverpool, walking in the dusky city toward a circle of light. There was a pool, and in the middle of the pool an island. In the middle of the island was a magnolia tree. It stood in the sunlight and at the same time was the source of that light. He drew the magnolia flower in the center of his mandala.

Often in my journal, I draw a very simple mandala with a pencil, placing an image from a dream or from my surroundings in the center and letting my imagination fill the space around it. Sometimes I draw the image multiple times, letting it circle around the center, and other times it fills the entire mandala. I call my mandalas soul maps and I give them titles. When I go back to my journal and look at one of my mandalas, I can feel where I was at the moment of drawing it. The mandalas are signposts along my path.

Here is a mandala I drew of a pear blossom, several years back when I first started to include mandalas in my journal. We had recently moved. I was writing in my journal and looking at a pear tree we had transplanted from our old house. I was hoping it would take root and bring forth large lovely white blossoms. I drew one blossom, first penciling in the dark seeds at the center and then drawing the flower with five petals. As I looked at the seeds, the petals slowly multiplied; instead of five, I drew ten, and then fifteen, reaching outward to the circumference of the mandala.

Pear Blossom
Bellevue, June, 1999

So now, in this chapter on journaling, I ask you to draw a mandala. Take a sheet of paper and draw a circle of a size that feels comfortable to you. Look at your circle and draw a circle in its center. Place your image in the center circle. Or let it circle around the center. Fill up the rest of the space as you wish, with circles, lines, images. Don't worry about your drawing. Just enjoy the exercise: let yourself draw, let yourself play.

✎ Exercise: Draw a mandala, letting your image lead you.
   Ten minutes.

Look at your mandala and give it a title. Take your time doing this. Think of how we name our children, how long we spend mulling over possible first names. When we name something, we acknowledge it. This is your drawing: give it a name.

WRITING THE STORY OF THE JOURNAL IMAGE

I noted that one of the reasons to journal is to plant seeds for stories. What is your image's story? You have described your image in a journal entry and drawn it in a mandala. What story is this image unfolding?

Here is the story I wrote about my pear tree, crafted as a prose poem, from *Circling to the Center*. This precedes the white pear blossom I drew. I was still living in our old house, sitting at my desk and looking out the window at the scrawny pear tree with skimpy blossoms in our front yard. It made me think about my mother-in-law suffering from Alzheimer's, bent and crippled, strapped into a wheelchair in a nursing home. On my desk was a postcard I had just received of Vincent van Gogh's *Pear Tree in Bloom*. His pear tree's size and shape were strikingly similar to the size and shape of mine. Both were skinny and crooked, even leaning in the same direction. But the blossoms on Van Gogh's pear tree were immense, and I realized that the glory of the blossoms depended upon who was looking at them.

"Pear Tree"

Outside my window, in the middle of our front yard, leans a small pear tree. The trunk is dark gray. It puts out blossoms, skimpy ones on skinny branches. I wanted it out of sight. Planted many years ago, it grew crooked even with its wooden stake. When I finally pulled away the stake, I feared for its anorexic branches.

My husband's mother, stricken with Alzheimer's disease, sits strapped to a wheelchair, a woolen scarf tight across her chest. Her face is dazed in disbelief. Her eyes are dark gray circles. I look for light in them and find darkness. Her fingers try to fasten the last button on her sweater.

Today a postcard of van Gogh's painting *Pear Tree in Bloom* arrived. Its dark gray trunk is twisted, the branches ugly and crippled. But in the gnarled fists, there are bunches of color, mandalas of white blossoms, surrounded with a few dark leaves.

The image of the pear tree led me to my mother-in-law and to the glorious blossoms on van Gogh's pear tree. From there it led me to look for mandalas of white blossoms on my own tree, and in my mother-in-law's dark eyes. And a few years later it led me to my pear tree flower mandala, from the dark seeds in the center to the multiplying white blossoms.

Now start to shape the story of your image into a piece of writing. Write perhaps just one paragraph. Think of yourself as a potter; the clay is your image. For the clay to become a jug, it needs your hands. So does the image: to unfold its story, it needs your words.

✎ Exercise: Shape the story of your image into a piece of writing. Ten minutes. And remember to give it a title.

JOURNALING TO THE CORE

Now let's look at another book written as a journal, May Sarton's *Journal of A Solitude,* in which Sarton speaks of reaching down to the matrix, to the core of her being, where there are emotions hidden away. In *Writing a Woman's Life,* Carolyn Heilbrun says that the publication of Sarton's book in

1973 was a turning point for modern women's autobiography. Several years earlier, Sarton had published *Plant Dreaming Deep,* a beautiful account of her adventure of buying a house and living alone. Only afterward, as she received letters from readers wishing to follow her example and go live alone in New England, did she realize that she had concealed her rage and despair as she idealized her solitary life. She had written her story in the old romantic genre of female autobiography, romanticizing her life. She wrote *Journal of a Solitude* to deliberately record her anger and isolation.

SEPTEMBER 15TH

Begin here. It is raining. I look out on the maple, where a few leaves have turned yellow, and listen to Punch, the parrot, talking to himself and to the rain ticking gently against the windows. I am here alone for the first time in weeks, to take up my "real" life again at last . . .

Plant Dreaming Deep has brought me many friends of the work (and also, harder to respond to, people who think they have found in me an intimate friend). But I have begun to realize that, without my own intention that book gives a false view. The anguish of my life here—its rages—is hardly mentioned. Now I hope to break through into the rough rocky depths, to the matrix itself. There is violence there and anger never resolved. . . . My need to be alone is balanced against my fear of what will happen when suddenly I enter the huge empty silence . . .

A matrix is something within which something else originates or develops. It is the natural material in which a fossil, gem, or crystal is embedded. Sarton is showing how to go deeper, how to break through to the rough, rocky depths within to the matrix itself. She invites you, the reader, to go down to the matrix, to the huge empty silence where your creativity is embedded.

As a final exercise, write another journal entry that reaches down deep within you, one that is not afraid to express anger and frustration. What do you truly feel today? As you release your feelings, let them flow into words, words that come from your center, the core. Write as deeply as you can. Start with the date, and this time with May Sarton's words, "Begin here . . ."

✎ Exercise: Write a second journal entry, reaching toward the depths within. Ten minutes. Look for a new title to help ground your second entry.

When you write this way, you open to your inner world. You take something visible and let it lead you to the invisible. You become a bridge between the two worlds, a bridge for yourself, discovering a deeper self, and a bridge for those around you, discovering together your shared humanity.

✎ There are five exercises in this lesson. They may be done as you read the lesson, one after another. Or you can spread them out, focusing on one exercise each week. In the latter case, you can do the first journal entry the first week, the description of the image and the mandala together the second week. The third week you can write the story of your image. And the last week, write the second journal entry.

Personal Essays

W hen Robert Atwan published the first *Best American Essays* in 1986, it was a gamble in the world of letters. Atwan did not know when he would have enough good essays for another collection. Not only has the series continued every year since, but other anthologies have joined the ranks, and the essay continues to flourish. Once a "second class citizen" (according to E.B. White), the essay today finds a regular home in periodicals ranging from *The New Yorker* to *Creative Nonfiction,* from *The Atlantic Monthly* to *Fourth Genre,* from *Newsweek* to *The Sun* to *The Christian Science Monitor.* And it has migrated, shifting its shape into other kinds of nonfiction writing, from editorials and travel pieces to journals and profiles, to commentaries and memoirs. "The essay is all over the map," writes Annie Dillard, "there is nothing you cannot do with it, no subject matter is forbidden, no structure is proscribed."

In these different shapes and suits, the essay is the primary short unit of longer nonfiction works. When Natalie Goldberg wrote *Writing Down the Bones,* she wrote each chapter as a self-contained essay. When Alice Walker wrote her nonfiction book *Anything We Love Can Be Saved,* many of the chapters had first appeared as individual essays. And Kathleen Norris wrote most of the text of *Dakota* in the essay form, adding journal entries, poems, and weather reports. The same observation holds true for Stephen King in his book *On Writing.* It is written in fragments. King calls them snapshots, occasional memories "against a fogged-out landscape."

In this second lesson, you will write snapshots. Often, the subject for your essay will be found in your journal entries—those moments when, as you reread your journals, you stop and think, Here is the seed of an essay. This is an important practice as you move into a writing life. Your journals are gardens. Return to them to find what is ready to flourish.

INTRODUCTION TO CREATIVE NONFICTION

Before we go further into the history, components, and structure of the essay, let's look at this broad spectrum of nonfiction that we now call creative nonfiction. The term itself was first used by the National Endowment for the Arts in the 1970s to describe the new journalism that was being done by writers like Truman Capote (*In Cold Blood,* 1965), Joan Didion (*Slouching Towards Bethlehem,* 1968), and Gay Talese (*Honor Thy Father,* 1971). These writers were adapting fictional techniques to reporting. Capote's first intention was to do a series for *The New Yorker* on the four shotgun murders of the Clutter family in Kansas in 1959. But when he traveled there, met and spoke with neighbors, friends, policemen, and jurors, and talked at length with the two accused murderers, he was no longer writing a journalistic piece, but one of personal experience and exploration.

In *The Art of Creative Nonfiction,* Lee Gutkind describes four techniques to master in writing this genre.

— Embellish description. Do not manipulate accuracy, but enhance the dramatic impact of your characters and your setting.
— Use dialogue. Recreate conversations as you remember them, but not conversations that did not happen.
— Include inner point of view. Let the reader see the world as you see it, through your eyes.
— Capture the subject in scenes. Scenes are action oriented, cinematic, and three-dimensional. They are pictures built with intimate details that entice the reader into the piece.

In this way the creative nonfiction writer uses all the literary techniques available to the fiction writer in order to render his story as compelling as possible, but he does not invent. As a nonfiction writer you are writing about what you experienced, not what you fabricate. John McPhee insists that nonfiction writers have a real obligation to one another and to their readers: credibility. You cannot exactly reproduce people's lives, but it is important to get as close as you can to what you see and hear.

In 1995 Lee Gutkind founded the review *Creative Nonfiction* to showcase the vitality and excellence of this flourishing new genre of writing. In 1999 Michael Steinberg started the review

Fourth Genre, adding to the recognized literary canon of three genres—fiction, poetry, and drama—nonfiction as the fourth. Bret Lott writes in "Toward a Definition of Creative Nonfiction" (Spring 2000 issue of *Fourth Genre*) that this genre of writing comes from the self: the self is the continent and the writer is its first explorer. But creative nonfiction can never be self-serving. Instead it opens out to the ever-expanding world, where the writer takes responsibility for his words.

THE PERSONAL ESSAY

The essay is the basic short form of nonfiction. A brief history of the essay would start in the late sixteenth century with Montaigne writing *essays* (endeavors), letting the subjective and the objective intertwine into a new form of prose. Montaigne was a retired lawyer, a gentleman farmer living on his family estate in Dordogne. To keep himself busy, he started writing essays, addressing whatever subject was close to him and writing in whatever form suited his immediate fancy. He believed "Each man bears the entire form of man's estate," hence his writings might be of interest to all. His essays were conversations with an unseen neighbor. When we read them, we feel he is talking to us, directly and freely. He is giving us his point of view. We come away both refreshed and enlightened.

As we skip to the twentieth century, Virginia Woolf speaks of the essay as a balance of subject and style, with each component being equally important. Above all, "the essay has as its backbone, a fierce attachment to truth." Philip Lopate describes the essay as a conversation between the writer and the reader as "one individual speaking to another who wants to listen."

How should we define the personal essay, also called the

informal or literary essay? In the foreword to the 1988 *Best American Essays,* Robert Atwan notes that writers are coming to the essay with growing enthusiasm because of its malleability. He points to four components of the personal essay: voice, form, drama, and truth.

1. Voice: The essay has a personal voice and is written in first person. It is not enough to render an experience; the writer has to give his or her perspective. As a writer you need not be afraid to say what you think. You can turn to Doris Lessing, who writes in *The Golden Notebook* that the way to deal with the problem of subjectivity is to see each individual as a microcosm, and to transform a private experience into something larger, making the personal general. If you honestly share an experience that you have lived deeply, it will touch the reader. It will move from the personal to the universal.

2. Form: The essay lives along the border of fiction and poetry. This is also true for the memoir (which will be discussed in a later lesson). Here the writer relates her experience in the form of a story and polishes it as she would a poem. The story keeps the statement unobtrusive. The poetry expands the meaning. This balancing between story and poem is what makes the essay so inventive—agile (shaping itself into an astonishing variety of forms) yet incisive (revealing a passionate engagement with one's material).

3. Drama: As Dillard wrote, no subject is proscribed. The whole world offers itself as subject—as long as the

subject is dramatic. This is not the strict, old-fashioned essay once taught in school. Atwan recounts that when he read one of Dillard's essays to a group of students, they claimed that it was not an essay, saying it had too much drama for an essay. But personal essays are narrated from real life. And real life is drama. The writer has experienced it.

4. Truth: The essay leaves both the writer and the reader with a truth. Here is the fierce backbone that Virginia Woolf wrote about. A story does not necessarily leave the reader with a truth. But an essay must. This is one of the big differences between short story and essay. It is often said that an essay is a short story in disguise and vice versa, a short story is an essay in disguise. But no. An essay relates something that happened and it offers the author's insight into the meaning of it. It's not enough to show; you have to tell. As Robert Atwan says in "The Return of the Essay," "What essays give you is a mind at work."

In her introduction to *Best American Essays 2001*, Kathleen Norris writes that a genuine essay feels like a dialogue between writer and reader. After reading the first paragraph, the reader concludes that he wants to listen. The essay will tell him something about the world that he didn't know before. It will give him a thought, a memory, an emotion made richer by the experience of the essayist. Norris is claiming here that resonance is the key.

So how does the essayist do this? Let's look at a carefully crafted essay. Here is a short personal essay from *Fourth Genre* (Spring 2001) written by George R. Clay relating what would seem a banal experience.

"Where Everything Begins"

This is something that happened the other morning—Thursday, June 9. At about 11:30. Something quite wonderful, considering it was really nothing much.

I thought that trash was picked up on Wednesdays here in Cambridge, but apparently not. Anyway, I turned off Mass. Ave. onto Lee Street, looking for a parking space, and found myself stuck behind the city garbage truck. Lee is a side street, one way. Cars parked on both curbs. You can't pass anyone. The trash truck was bright orange, called The Works. Two men were picking up, toting, dumping—one each side of the street. The man working the west side (to my left) was small, silver-haired, silver-rimmed glasses. Assistant-clerkish, except for bulging forearms and a don't-eyeball-me look on his face. The other was monstrous ugly, in a nice way: a cross between Jaws (in the James Bond movies) and Fernandel. Long, slouchy, strong, lazy-limbed body. Took his time with the containers, lifting them with slow grace, never slamming anything or tipping it in anger. Though there was distasteful expression on his face, a "this job literally stinks" look. After taking care of half Lee Street's east side, he paused outside a house with a garden. Looked up and down the brick sidewalk to make sure he wasn't being watched; checked the house windows; then, with care and determination, lifted his long right leg and hopped into the middle of the deep street-front portion of the garden—mostly big flat leaves, but colored blossoms too (marigolds? I couldn't tell). He crouched down, down, further down, and suddenly plunged his face into the biggest leaves and breathed— inhaled them, not coming up for at least half a minute. When he did, his expression betrayed nothing, neither pleasure nor guilt nor watchfulness. With a poker face he stood, backed considerably out of the garden, and returned to his work. I thought that Flannery O'Connor had got it right—this is where everything begins: with the senses.

This is a story that makes you, the reader, feel richer. How does Clay put you behind a city garbage truck to learn that the story begins with the senses? Let's look at the four components.

Voice: Clay is speaking to you; something happened this morning, he says. Not much, but very wonderful. As a reader, you begin instantly to trust this voice, like that of a friend speaking to you.

Form: The essay follows a clear narrative. There is the story—all in one paragraph, starting with the bright orange garbage truck. And there are the poetic details—the two men, the small man with silver hair and silver-rimmed glasses, and the long, slouchy, lazy-limbed larger man. Look at the alliteration (the repetition of consonant sounds), the s's and the l's. The story continues, one action after another, each detail carefully crafted.

Drama: As reader you see at first a banal story, but when the long, lazy-limbed guy looks up and down the sidewalk, and then bends down low, still lower, you are caught. What is he doing? Until suddenly he plunges his face into the biggest leaves and inhales for at least half a minute. The long guy has won your sympathy.

Truth: Clay is fierce here. The man returns to his work, poker-faced, but restored. Clay takes the reader to Flannery O'Connor: everything begins with the senses.

Clay has worked with each of the four elements to write a personal essay that both captivates and instructs.

Here is another example, this time from the journal *Creative Nonfiction* (Number 27, 2005), a short essay by Bret Lott, "Genesis."

"GENESIS"

I am sitting in the sanctuary, a few rows from the front: to my left, my mom, my dad and my little brother, Timmy, in Mom's lap, sleeping; to my right, my older brother, Brad. Brad and I have just received these thin, blue books, every kid in the service passed a brand new copy by men in gray or black suits standing at either end of the pews, stacks of these books in hand.

The blue paper cover is bordered with green grapevines, tendrils working up and down either side, with bunches of grapes here and there; at the top and bottom of the cover, those tendrils meet sheaves of wheat in the same green ink.

The pastor says it is the book of somms, and I wonder what that is, look at the words in black ink centered a little high on the cover. I sound out the words to myself: *The Book of*—and stop.

P-S-A-L-M-S. How does that, I wonder, spell out somms?

But even if I don't understand, this is the first Bible—or piece of it—I have ever gotten, and I don't want to lose this book. I want to keep it.

So I take one of the nubby pencils from the back of the pew in front of me, nestled in its tiny wooden hole beside the wooden shelf where attendance forms are kept, and beside the larger holes where the tiny glass cups are placed once we've emptied them of grape juice.

And I begin, for the first time in my life, to write my name by myself.

I start in the upper left-hand corner, just below the border, but the first word trails off, falls toward that centered title in black, as though that title is a magnet and the letters I make are iron filings. They fall that way because there are no lines for me to balance them upon, as I am able to do on the paper given me by my kindergarten teacher, Mrs. Pasley.

I finish that first word, feel in my hand the cramp of so much strenuous, focused work, and hold the book away from me, look at it while the pastor rolls on.

There is no place for the second word; the last letter of my first name is too near the first of the title.

This is a problem. I know the second word must follow the first word on the same line, a little space needed between them. Mrs. Pasley would not approve. This is a problem.

But there is a space above my name due to its falling away and I write, work out the riddles of letters without lines, letters that will line up to mark this book as mine and mine only.

Then I am finished, and here is my name. Me.

The first time I have ever written my name myself, alone.

Later on the way home, my older brother, Brad, will look at the book, say, "Lott Bret. Who's that?" and laugh at my ill-spaced effort. Later still I will write my name again on the cover, this time with a blue pen and holding the book upside down. The words will be a little more jaunty, full of themselves and the confidence of a kid who knows how to write his name, no problem at all. Beneath this second round, though, will be the lone letter *B* a practice swing at making that capital letter as good as I can make it.

Later I will be baptized into the church at age 14, a ritual that, it seems to me, is the right thing to do.

Later still, in college, I will be born again, as Christ instructed Nicodemus.

And later even still, I will have written entire books of my own, created lives out of the whole cloth of the imagination. I will have created, and created in my name.

But on this Sunday, with the pastor still rolling on, these two words are enough.

Only a kid's scrawl. My own small imitation of God.

As you asked yourself with the first essay, how does Bret Lott draw you into that sanctuary where he will have his first experience of selfhood? A memory from childhood. Look again at the four components of a good essay:

Voice: In first person, an adult remembers how as a child he wanted to write his own name alone, how he wanted to be his own creator. The voice is direct and honest.

Form: Lott tells a story; there are colorful details, a bit of suspense, some tension with his brother, resolution. And there are elements of poetry, images, the tendrils of green grapevines, the title of the book a magnet, the simile, and the letters as iron fillings, the repetition five times of the word "later."

Drama: A childhood memory takes on resonance as you associate yourself with this little child wanting so earnestly to write his name, to be creative, foreshadowing the author he would become.

Truth: Bret Lott names his first book with a kid's scrawl, his own imitation of God. The whole scene is so aptly titled "Genesis." It is a lesson about the origin of self-consciousness.

Lott has crafted a personal essay—a personal experience—that will remain in the reader's mind. It is an experience that is familiar to you, but Lott has shown it in a new light.

FOUR STEPS TO WRITING A PERSONAL ESSAY

How do you write your own personal essay? You can do it in four steps; each step is a new draft, a new version. I have been teaching these steps for over fifteen years now, and I have also followed them in writing my own essays. Don't write yet; first read through the steps and the example that follows.

1. Choose and Tell

Choose an experience, or rather, let it choose you. What experience do you want to write about? Close your eyes, go within, and let the experience find you. Spend a few moments resting with your eyes closed, listening deep within. What experience, what memory of a person, a place, an event, an insight, an emotion, wants to be written about? What memory surfaces? Let it find you.

When the experience makes itself known, focus and frame it in your mind like a photo: not everything, but the important part of the experience. Montaigne wrote, "Everything has one hundred parts, one hundred faces, I take one of them . . . I do not paint it as wide as I can but I jab into it as deep as I can."

If you are in a workshop setting, share your memory with the person sitting next to you. Does it catch the person's attention? If you start too early in the story of your memory, it will lose momentum. If you give too many details, interest will wander. If the person looks bored, then start anew; wait for another experience to choose you.

If you are not in a workshop, try to catch the experience in a few words, like a snapshot: be spontaneous. Just a paragraph. Take a breath and read what you have written. See if it interests you. Find a friend to read it to and see how she reacts. If you or your friend are uninterested, start anew.

When the memory has caught the attention of your listener (or yours if you are alone), write a first draft. Freewrite. Do not control this first draft. Let the essay meander to another subject. Meander is a good word for essay writing. As you write about an experience, one thought leads to another and you meander as a river does, diverging, digressing, winding from the source to a final outlet.

2. Show

Now show the experience in a second draft. Show what happened by writing in scenes. Joyce Carol Oates writes that the older essay form is more rhetorical, whereas the newer is much more cinematic. And remember the importance of the first sentence. Does it interest the reader? Do the first words catch the reader?

Think about the elements of story telling:

— Specific details of setting and characters
— Tension and dialogue
— Plotting: a narrative tug
— Revelation/resolution (The protagonist, the "I" of the essay, has to discover something.)

Depending upon the subject, do some research. Bring the reader new information. And always bring a new perspective from your own reflections. In *The Art of the Personal Essay* Philip Lopate writes that an essay has a rise and fall. It digs up something and reaches deeper understandings than it began with.

This will be a second draft—thinking story, thinking scenes.

3. Polish

Slowly start to polish your words. In this third step, you are adding resonance to your essay, as poets do with their work.

Think about the elements of poetry:

— Imagery. Reread your essay and look for the images. Images are anything that you can draw. Circle them. Are some of them crafted as similes (images introduced with the words "like" or "as") and others as metaphors (without "like" or "as")? Hold on to one of the images. If it is a simile, write it as a metaphor. Expand it. Let it summon up a deeper meaning. This way it becomes a symbol, a visible sign of something invisible.

— Rhythm and sound. Now listen to your essay. Read it aloud. Find repetitions of words, of sounds (alliteration, the repetition of consonant sounds, and assonance, the repetition of vowel sounds). Find words that sound like what they describe (an easy way to define the word "onomatopoeia"). And listen to the melody, more technically to the meter, to the rhythm of the stressed syllables and the unstressed. Does it flow? Seamus Heaney calls this element "the voltage of poetry."

— Compression: And finally, consider the element of compression. What is the core of the experience? What is its truth? In "Burnt Norton," T.S. Eliot speaks of the still point of the turning world. Where is the still point of your essay? By compressing, you distill the experience. You discover its essence.

This will be a third draft.

4. Wait and Then Bring Forth

Set your essay aside, at least overnight—better still, for several nights or even weeks. It takes me a good month to write a personal essay. In *Letters to a Young Poet,* Rainer Maria Rilke writes "Everything is gestation, then bringing forth." Be patient. Let your work ripen.

If you have the good fortune to have a writers' group, share the essay. Listen to what others have to suggest. If you don't have a writers' group, share it with a friend. Share it with yourself: read it aloud. Listen to it.

Then revise (to see again): Does your essay say what you hoped it would? Or does it need serious revision? Do not be discouraged; instead, be grateful for the opportunity to strengthen your work. We will look at length at revision in Lesson Eleven.

When you are ready, consider looking for a home for your essay. The pursuit of publishing is a book in itself. Resources abound, online and in print, and I offer some guidelines at the end of this book. For now, be certain that if in the writing you have discovered something fresh and unique in one of your life experiences, readers will share this discovery.

WRITING THE PERSONAL ESSAY

Pretend that you are following the four steps to write a story about going food shopping in Cambridge, Massachusetts. But remember—you first must actually go food shopping in Cambridge; you cannot make up the whole experience. This is the litmus test of nonfiction. The writer can embellish description, include dialogue, write in scenes, but the experience has to have happened.

Let me share my experience food shopping in Cambridge for my daughter and son-in-law and their three-day-old baby. Food shopping in a country where I had not lived for thirty years, but a country filled with people who looked like me and spoke like me. In my first draft (step one), it was a distressing experience. I had felt misunderstood, out of place. In the second draft (step two), I started to make it into a story. I included some of the dialogue, highlighting the humor and tension. I moved toward a revelation. For the third draft, I polished the images, paid attention to the rhythm, and used repetition. And the truth of the experience? Well, let me ask you. Here is the story, as it appeared in a "Meanwhile" column in *The International Herald Tribune*.

"In a Grocery Far from Home"

"Plastic or paper, lady?" asked the young man with a pony tail, as I was looking in my purse for enough cash to pay for the groceries.

It was summer vacation, and I had returned to the States to become a new grandmother.

"May I pay with my American Express card?" I said to the woman at the register, not yet ready to tackle the option of plastic or paper.

"No, Ma'am, only Visa or Masters."

"And a check?"

"With two identification cards, Ma'am," she answered,

handing me the stub. Her fingernails were longer than I remembered ever seeing and painted brilliant pink. "Do you have a driver's license?"

I started to fill out the check. "I have a driver's license but it's Swiss."

The young man who had asked me about plastic or paper eyed me with curiosity. He had three earrings of different lengths all on the same ear.

"What did you say dear?" asked the cashier.

The line behind me was getting longer, but it was also getting interested.

"I said my license is Swiss. I don't live here, I live in Switzerland."

Everyone turned toward me. If only I had a hint of a foreign accent, no one would have paid attention. This was Cambridge, Massachusetts, where in summertime one out of two people speaks a foreign language. But my English sounded like their English. Where did I come from? I looked American, I spoke American, but I didn't perform American.

"Let me see dear. I don't want to make you trouble."

Again the young man asked, "Plastic or paper, lady?"

Lady? I thought I was a woman. What was this lady business? And ma'am? And dear?

"Honey, he just means how do you want it wrapped? In a plastic bag or in a paper bag."

I had such a large, attentive audience that I found the question difficult. Which was more ecological? Making paper bags destroyed the trees and forests. But was the plastic bio-whatever? I made a wish that the plastic be whatever it should be and said, "Plastic, please."

The young man snapped open a large bag and placed it on

a frame at the end of the checkout counter where it sat suspended.

"Your license please, and another piece of identity."

All this hassle for $22.20. I thought about giving the groceries back, but my daughter and French son-in-law were waiting for them—one romaine lettuce, three red apples (they were so polished I squished one just a little to see if it were real), sharp cheddar cheese, and steak (painstakingly chosen among meters—I mean yards—of packaged steaks). I couldn't give it all back, it was to be our dinner.

So out came my Swiss driver's license, written in French, with a photo of me about twenty years back, well, maybe thirty. The cashier looked at me and then back at the photo. Skepticism. Next came my American passport, recently renewed, like one month ago. Mistrust. Grandmothers do age.

She rang for the manager, her bright pink fingernail poised on the bell.

I waited. The young man packing my groceries waited. The people in line waited. No one murmured, no one was impatient. This too was different. I could even hear the air conditioners.

When the manager, dressed in a gray pinstripe suit arrived, I was so confused I reached out to shake his hand. I was ready to apologize.

"Is this all right?" I asked, pushing the check, the Swiss driver's license, the American passport in his direction.

"Yes. Everything is fine." He smiled and wrote his signature on the back of my check. I could feel the wave of general relief.

"You know," he said, "I always dreamed of going to Switzerland."

What is the truth? What did I discover in writing about food shopping in Cambridge?

I discovered that the small grocery store in Cambridge where my daughter lived with her husband and new-born baby, was welcoming me back home. The woman calling me "dear" and "honey," the young man waiting with his bags, the people waiting in the line behind me, and the manager in his pinstriped suit—they all wanted to make me feel comfortable. I was finally not a stranger. We shared one common humanity.

Now it's your turn. Return to the first three steps as you write a personal essay of about seven hundred words, about the length of the short essay "Plastic or Paper." Something that you can work on for three spurts of writing, ten minutes each.

First step: Choose and Tell. Lean back and close your eyes. What experience wants to be written about? When you have found it (when it has found you), focus on it, get rid of the extra bits, and frame it. Where are you going to start? If you are in a group of writers, share the experience with the person next to you. See if he is interested. Find another experience if necessary. If you're not in a group, try sharing your experience with a friend or family member. See if it holds her attention. Or try capturing the experience in a few sentences, like a snapshot, and see if it catches your own interest. Then, remembering to focus and frame first, start writing.

✎ Exercise: Free-write. Go wherever the experience takes you. Do not edit or cross out. Fifteen minutes.

Second step: Show. Now think story. Write your memory in scenes—perhaps just one scene for a short essay. Look at your first sentence. Is this where the essay should begin? Will it grab the reader's interest? Find a few specific details about setting and characters. Try to remember some dialogue and add it to create tension. Think about the resolution. What are you discovering in this experience?

✎ Exercise: Rewrite the essay, a second draft with
   elements of story. Go more slowly. Fifteen minutes.

Third step: Polish. Now think poetry, think lyrical. Look at images. As you did in Lesson One with your journal entries, reread and circle images. Find an image that can be described with a simile. Copy it and see if you can work it into a metaphor. Does it reach deeper to something within? Next look at sounds. Read your first paragraph aloud. How is the rhythm? If your voice catches somewhere, go back and smooth it out. Is there repetition of sounds? Alliteration (repetition of consonant sounds)? Assonance (repetition of vowel sounds)? Polish the first sentences.

✎ Exercise: Rewrite the essay, your third draft, with elements of poetry. Work perhaps on just the first paragraph. Fifteen minutes. Now give your essay a title.
   Naming is always important; it centers the essay on your
   page and in your writing.

Fourth Step: Wait and bring forth. Now you have the beginning of a personal essay, and you have worked to craft it. When you have more time, go back to the second and third steps. Hone your essay as a story. Polish it as a poem. What is its truth? Then take the fourth step: let it sit for a while before going back to it. Now look at it again and do some rewriting. Share it with others and work to revise it. Remember, this is re-visioning.

To conclude this chapter on the personal essay I return to Annie Dillard, as did Robert Atwan in celebrating the twentieth volume of *The Best American Essay* series. He wrote that Dillard put it perfectly in the 1988 collection when she observed that the essay had joined the modern world. "The essay," Dillard wrote, "can do everything a poem can do, and everything a short story can do—everything but fake it." This is the attraction of the essay, for both the writer and the reader. It is yours to enjoy.

✎ This chapter includes three timed exercises and a longer fourth, when you return to your essay and craft it further with the elements of story and poem. The first three—free-writing the first draft, rewriting with elements of story, and polishing with elements of poetry—may be done one after the other as you read the lesson. Or you may devote more time to each, especially to the second and third. Then when it feels right, go on to the last step to finish your essay.

WRITING THE ESSAY
(Four Steps—Four Levels)

1. Choose and tell (first level essay)

    —Choose an experience (let it choose you): an event, place, observation, emotion

    —Focus and frame ("Everything has one hundred faces, I take one of them . . ."—Montaigne)

    —Gather information (put experience in perspective, intersection with public life)

    —Free-write first draft ("Essays meander and tell anecdotes as they disclose."—Michael Depp)

2. Show (second level essay)

    —Show what happened, write in scenes ("The older [essay] form is more rhetorical, the newer is much more cinematic."—Joyce Carol Oates)

    —Dramatize: (elements of story writing)

    (1) setting and characters (embellish description, specific details)

    (2) tension (through action and dialogue, heightening of intensity)

    (3) climax / plotting ("a rise and a fall as it digs up something"—Lopate)

    (4) revelation / resolution (protagonist discovers something)

    —Write a second draft, thinking elements of story

3. Polish (third level essay)

  —Move from the individual to the universal ("See the tiny individual as a microcosm . . . transforming the private experience into something much larger." Dorris Lessing), making resonant the deeper meaning

  —Amplify (elements of poetry writing)

    (1) images (similes, metaphors, symbols)

    (2) sounds (rhythm, melody, voltage: alliteration, assonance, repetition)

    (3) compression, distillation ("At the still point of the turning world . . ." —T.S. Eliot)

  —Write a third draft, thinking elements of poetry

4. Wait and then bring forth (fourth level essay)

  —Be patient ("Everything is gestation, then bringing forth." —Rilke)

  —Revise (see anew): leads/endings, details, tension, dialogue, imagery, rhythm, themes

  —Edit: length, sentence/paragraph structure, active verbs, unnecessary words, visual effect

  —Critique (value of writers' groups, workshops)

  —Market: networking, tools ("The essay is all over the map . . ." —Annie Dillard)

Opinion and Travel Essays

This lesson will help you make the transition from personal essays to opinion and travel essays. Because of its flexibility, the personal essay gives you the basic form with which to craft both opinion and travel pieces. The news article—fast and factual—used to be the accepted form for writing about our opinions and our travels. But today, as Robert Atwan, editor of *The Best American Essays,* explains, writers have discovered the essay in order to deal intelligently with the topics of their time in such a way that they may still be read with pleasure when the moment has passed.

INTRODUCTION TO THE OPINION ESSAY

Opinion essays sway hearts and change minds. They find their place as op-eds—a label derived from where they are found:

opposite the editorial pages—in newspapers (from the *New York Times* and the *Boston Globe* to your local newspaper), as commentary in magazines (such as *Newsweek, The Nation,* and *Harpers*), and as viewpoints on the vast, ever-growing World Wide Web (*Atlantic Monthly's Post & Riposte, Orion,* etc.). Op-eds are short and reach a very wide audience, from the *New York Times* with its circulation of l .7 million to local newspapers, such at Hackensack, New Jersey's *The Record,* with a circulation of 200,000. Commentary tends to be longer. The audience, depending upon the publication, is often very wide. "My Turn" essays in *Newsweek* reach a circulation of 3 million. Viewpoints online range from very short to very long, and the readership is limitless.

As a writer, you want to share not only stories and experiences, but also your opinions. You can write about a variety of topics, from politics and culture to family and gardens. In contributing op-eds and commentaries, you take your place in the public discourse. An op-ed is different from an article. Articles are time-bound and place-bound; in five years, they will be less interesting. Op-eds are neither time-bound nor place-bound. Although they very often address a timely subject and are specifically located, their interest is not as news but as opinion. In five years, well thought and well written op-eds will still attract attention.

In writing and contributing opinion essays, you the writer not only send your voice into the world, but you gain practice for other publishing endeavors. Writing succinct but pleasurable prose is excellent practice. Being concise is key. Newspaper op-eds generally range from five hundred to eight hundred words. Opinion essays in magazines range from eight hundred words upward. The "My Turn" essays in *Newsweek* and the "Lives" essays in the *New York Times Sunday Magazine* are nine hundred to a thousand words.

What are editors looking for? Here is what David Shipley at the *New York Times* writes in its guidelines: "We look for timeliness, ingenuity, strength of argument, freshness of opinion, clear writing and newsworthiness. Personal experience and first-person narrative can be great, particularly when they're in service of a larger idea."

In the guidelines for *The Christian Science Monitor* Kendra Nordin notes, "The Op-Ed page provides a forum for opinion and commentary on politics, the family, society and culture. . . . If it's a subject people care about and it's well written, we'd probably be interested in seeing it."

David Jarmul of the National Academy Op-ed Service adds, "Editors, without exception, prefer a gripping personal narrative from a local drug dealer to yet another ponderous analysis of the federal budget deficit. . . . The best subjects are those that readers care about."

So how do you find those subjects that readers care about and that are in the service of a larger idea? You stay aware of timely issues and write about what you are keenly interested in. If you are passionate in your writing, readers will be passionate in their reading. For example, if you fervently want to hand down to your children and grandchildren a world that is free of nuclear weapons, you first do research in the field, perhaps you participate in movements to ban nuclear armaments, and then you write about it. This is your commitment as a dedicated writer. Look again at the circulation figures for opinion pieces. Your words count.

THE OP-ED PUNCH

Essential to a good opinion piece is what I call the "op-ed punch." Short and decisive, the opinion piece must

— Grab attention (often through a gripping personal narrative)
— Resonate (speak directly to readers and ripple around them)
— Leave a truth (shed a new light on the subject)

These three elements are crucial to the successful delivery of an opinion essay.

Let's look at an example. Here is the beginning of an op-ed in *The International Herald Tribune,* in the Meanwhile Column, September 10, 2005, entitled "9/11 means heroism—and division," by Carie Lemack. The first sentences read: "It's hard to believe it has been four years since my mom was murdered on September 11, 2001. When my phone rings, I still find myself anticipating caller ID to pop up 'Mom cell.'"

Our attention is drawn immediately by the natural, almost familiar voice. The writer is sharing with the reader what happened to her mother. What will follow? Lemack moves beyond the conversations she could have with her mom. Instead, she imagines a conversation her mom could have with America's leaders, a conversation in which her mom would get the chance to tell them what her murder means.

Lemack is clear. Immediately following 9/11, the country came together as one giant family. But no longer. "September 11, which once united us, is now being used to divide us." Lemack flashes back to her childhood, remembering her mother's peacemaking between her sister and herself. Her mother made them hug and make up, reminding them that they would always be sisters and that was the most important thing. You the reader feel close to her as you remember similar experiences. It resonates.

Lemack concludes, asking Americans to come together again as one great nation: "Let's stop the internal warring going on in our own nation and come together to make it as great as it can be. Because, as my mom would remind our leaders, we are all Americans, and that is the most important thing." Lemack gives you something to think about. She casts a new light on how to protect our nation against future violence. She asks our leaders, and her readers, to remember that we are all Americans.

Here's another op-ed, from "My Turn" in *Newsweek* (July 28, 2003): "When Times Were Tough, We Went 'Bare'" by Sidney Stevens. It begins this way: "As my children, Kate and Alex, wobbled on skates to the rink and gingerly climbed onto the ice for the first time last January, my heart raced. 'Whatever you do,' I whispered, 'don't fall down.'"

Again, the reader is intrigued. Your attention is held. What is the writer worried about? Stevens explains right away. She is not an overprotective parent; she is worried about an accident and how to pay for a broken leg. Her husband has been laid off due to corporate reorganization, leaving them without health insurance. Stevens informs us that there are more than 41 million other uninsured Americans. She and her husband might be able to slide by until a job offer comes along, as long as no one slipped on the ice.

Then she receives a reminder about her yearly mammogram. The story ripples around you; again, the experience is familiar. Stevens walks into the mammography office "bare"—officially uninsured. When asked about her insurance, she feels ashamed, as though she has done something wrong. Her husband finally gets a job with health benefits, but Stevens is no longer complacent. It could happen again, and what about the millions who are still where she was?

A "My Turn" essay with an op-ed punch catches attention, resonates, and throws new light on the critical question of health insurance.

TIPS FOR WRITING OPINION ESSAYS

The op-ed punch is a quick test for checking the vitality of an opinion piece. Here is a list of tips to help you craft your own opinion essays.

— Write about something that is important to you and that you are qualified to speak about.
— Use your own voice in order to show why you care.
— Hook the reader with the first sentence.
— State your subject early to convince the reader that the essay is worth reading.
— Make a single point and make it well. Narrow the scope of the essay.
— Illustrate, with vivid examples and dialogue. One illustration is better than a hundred words.
— Use mostly short sentences and short paragraphs. Think visually.
— End well. Summarize your main point and return to the beginning.

A question to ask yourself as you are writing an op-ed is, "So what? Who cares?" You have a chance here to reach hundreds of thousands of readers. If the subject you have chosen is really important to you, each paragraph will build upon the reader's attention, whether the subject is of national importance or local interest. If you care enough about it, the reader will care.

Here is an example by Barbara Kingsolver, originally written as an op-ed in the *Los Angeles Times,* then expanded when Kingsolver gave it the chance to appear in her book, *Small Wonder.* In the foreword, Kingsolver tells us that in writing this book she learned that it is possible to move beyond an unbearable pain by delving into it deeper and deeper. We need this lesson. Here are the opening paragraphs of the essay from *Small Wonder.*

FROM THE ESSAY, "LIFE IS PRECIOUS, OR IT'S NOT"

"Columbine used to be one of my favorite flowers," my friend told me, and we both fell silent. We'd been talking about what she might plant on the steep bank at the foot of the woods above her house, but a single word cut us suddenly adrift from our focus on the uncomplicated life in which flowers could matter. I understood why she no longer had the heart to plant columbines. I feel that way too, and at the same time I feel we ought to plant them everywhere, to make sure we remember. In our backyards, on the graves of the children lost, even on the graves of the children who murdered, whose parents must surely live with the deepest emotional pain it is possible to bear.

In the aftermath of the Columbine High School shootings in Colorado, the whole country experienced grief and shock—and very noticeably—the spectacle of a nation acting bewildered. Even the op-ed commentators who usually tell us just what to think were asking, instead, what we should think. How could this happen in an ordinary school, an ordinary neighborhood? Why would any student, however frustrated with mean-spirited tormentors, believe that guns and bombs were the answer?

I'm inclined to think all of us who are really interested

in these questions might have started asking them a long
while ago . . .

Kingsolver develops her argument that the tragedy in Littleton
grew out of a culture that is rooting for the global shootout.
And for those looking for meaning, she wants to nail home a
benchmark. "Life is that precious, period." She ends her essay
with a summons to action. Remember "The children are paying
attention."

 Now look at how the tips mentioned above are respected in
this opinion piece.

— Write about something that is important to you: The
   tone of urgency in the essay persuades the reader of its
   importance both for the writer and the reader. Kingsolver's resolve does not waver.
— Use your own voice: Kingsolver speaks directly to the
   reader.
— Hook the reader with the first sentence: "'Columbine
   used to be one of my favorite flowers,' my friend told
   me, and we both fell silent." The conversation pulls the
   reader in immediately.
— State the subject early: Right in the first paragraph:
   ". . . to make sure we remember." Kingsolver will make
   the reader remember and will ask the reader to react.
— Make a single point: "Life is that precious, period."
— Illustrate: The essay starts with a conversation in a
   short scene.
— Think visually: The focus point, "Life is that precious,
   period" is in the next to last paragraph, driving home
   the argument.

— End well: Kingsolver returns to those she wishes to protect, the children.

She has written an op-ed that sways hearts and changes minds.

WRITING THE OPINION ESSAY

As we start to write an op-ed, let us return to the four steps for writing an essay from Lesson Two. We will work with the first two steps during this lesson.

First, choose and tell. What subject calls out to you? Let yourself be quiet and listen. It can be national, political, social, or environmental. It can be a current issue, even local if it is of general interest. It can also be a more personal subject—for instance a family celebration—as long as it has resonance. Once you have the subject, continue to reflect as you focus and frame. As in Lesson One, find someone to share your subject with. This is an effective way to focus and frame. Get the person's interest and keep it. Then start to write.

✎ Exercise: Free-write the first draft of your opinion piece. Ten minutes.

Now show (dramatize). Think about the elements of story. Think about a narrative tug and start the essay with a bit of dialogue and a strong emotion, as in Lemack's essay about 9/11, or with a good opening scene, as in Stevens' essay "When Times Were Tough" where she watches her children ice skating. Try to weave in dialogue; it enlivens and creates tension. Show—illustrate—why your opinion is important. Work on a second draft.

✎ Exercise: Write a second draft with a strong narrative tug. Fifteen minutes. And remember to stop for a moment to give your op-ed an attention-getting title.

You may work on the third step (polishing and making resonant) and fourth step (gestation and rewriting), on your own when you have more time, returning to the suggestions for these steps from Lesson Two.

Before we move on to writing travel essays, here are a few suggestions for when you are ready to submit an opinion essay to a newspaper or magazine. Be familiar with its style. Follow the submission guidelines, which are now posted on the web for most journals. The usual length is seven hundred words. The best op-ed markets to start with are hometown newspapers. Address your piece to the op-ed editor by name. Queries are usually not necessary. Brief cover letters are recommended when the writer has special expertise in the subject matter and/or clips (copies of published work).

And remember that one short opinion essay touches thousands of readers. This is how and where you take your place in the world as a writer, using your words to help make it a safer home for your children—for all children.

INTRODUCTION TO THE TRAVEL ESSAY

As is the case with the opinion essay, readers today want to have their minds and hearts captured when they read a travel essay. They look for essays that share the discovery of a place.

The now-outdated travel piece was filled with specific travel details: the length of the trip, the cost of the hotel, the menus, public transportation options, and so on. Today's travel essay brings the experience to life. If the editor wants to include service information, it is generally in a box to the side. Paul Theroux writes, "It is the intensity of the experience that matters." It is the journey itself that matters. And we do not need to travel far from home; a winner of *The Times* of London's travel essay contest several years back wrote about walking from his apartment to the newsstand on the street corner.

The editors of the magazine *Islands* have this to say to the travel writer in their guidelines: "We favor articles with a well-defined focus and point of view. Our purpose is, in effect, to take the reader to the island. We seek informative, insightful, personal pieces that reveal the essence of the place." What is important is what it feels like to be there.

Condé Nast Traveler suggests, "Paint a picture of the place you are writing about." Bring local color to your story, talk to the residents, and use quotes. *Condé Nast Traveler* in the United Kingdom looks in particular for travel articles that give an insight into personal experience.

Editor-in-chief Keith Bellows of *National Geographic Traveler* says that travelers want to be surprised. And he says to the travel writer, "A destination has to speak to you. You have to come back with a story. Travel is about stories."

Tom Cahill, guest editor of *The Best American Travel Writing,* 2006, writes, "Story is the essence of the travel essay. Stories are the way we orchestrate the voluminous factual material and—if we are very good—shed some light on the human condition."

From the editors of *Travelers' Tales,* anthologies of travel stories: "We're looking for personal, nonfiction stories and anecdotes—funny, illuminating, adventurous, frightening or grim. Stories should reflect that unique alchemy that occurs when you enter unfamiliar territory and begin to see the world differently as a result."

Personal stories in unfamiliar territory: how do you do this?

THREE ELEMENTS OF A TRAVEL ESSAY

To take the reader to a new place, the travel essay must be personal, imaginative, and informative.

First it must be personal, relating the writer's experience using the first person voice in such a way as to capture the reader's attention. The writer relates a unique, individual experience, and by sharing her own emotions and reactions, she touches the reader, moving beyond the individual to the universal. If I write about visiting the old Mayan capital Uxmal and its very steep Magician's Pyramid, I will write about my own experience: how, while trying to climb behind my husband, I was suddenly unable to move. Caught with vertigo, I could neither go up another step nor down. This personal account will resonate; the reader knows this feeling.

Second, good travel writing is imaginative. There is a story in the experience and the writer relates it and offers it to the reader. There is a narrative tug in a travel essay that opens up a new world. A Mexican woman is watching me. She sees that I am a foreigner, hears me speaking French to my husband, and she wants to help. She does not want me to go back to Europe without having climbed the Magician's Pyramid. She encourages me to descend slowly; she will show me another way.

Third, a travel essay is informative. There is reportage revealing the place, its history, its culture. The woman leads me to the back side of the pyramid where there is an easier staircase to a lower platform. She climbs the steps with me and we sit down under a giant mask of Chac, the god of rain. The Mayans were absolutely dependent upon rain. She points out the ruins of buried cisterns in the fields close by and recounts the legend of Chac.

Three different elements: personal, imaginative, informative. In this way the travel piece is part memoir (a personal experience), part story (imaginative, with a narrative tug), and part reportage (informative).

UNITIES OF GOOD TRAVEL WRITING

In his book *On Writing Well,* William Zinsser says that unity is the anchor of all good writing, especially travel writing, where the writer often goes off in different directions. Zinsser suggests the following choices for the travel writer.

— Unity of pronoun: Stay with the first person. Do not move into a third person writing as an observer. Remember that the reader sees the place through your experience. If you discover a statue of the Black Madonna in a chapel in the French Alps, relate how you saw the statue and how you felt standing in front of it. Do not drift into a long informative paragraph about Black Madonnas. Instead integrate the information into the story of your discovery.

— Unity of tense: Most travel essays are written in the simple past tense. "I opened the door to the chapel, and there in front of me was a dark statue of Mary, standing and staring at me . . ." Some writers are comfortable using the present tense. "I open the door to the chapel and there in front of me is a dark statue of Mary, standing and staring at me . . ." It is best to use one or the other and not switch back and forth. Sometimes, of course, the writer may need to move into a different tense to speak of something still further in the past or in the future, but he should choose one principal tense in which to address the reader.

— Unity of mood: The writer can use the casual voice of *The New Yorker,* or a more formal voice for a literary review. Both tones are acceptable, writes Zinsser, but don't mix the two. Don't begin a travel piece with a personal, reminiscent tone, "Let me tell you about my walk in the mountains. . ." then shift to a professorial tone, "On my daily afternoon walk, I discovered a deserted eighteenth-century chapel . . ." And still later to a guidebook style, "Above Saxel in Haute Savoie, there is an eighteenth-century chapel that is the home to a sixteenth-century statue of the Black Madonna . . ."

— Unity of subject: Narrow your lens. Do not try to talk about the French Alps, the architecture of the eighteenth century, and the statues of the Black Madonna. Take the reader to one place, one chapel, one statue. Remember what Montaigne said: "Everything has one hundred parts, one hundred faces, I take one of them . . ."

— Unity of thought: Not two or three thoughts, but one thought that will make the reader want to follow in your footsteps. Don't write about how to preserve the woods, about whether you are Catholic or not, about what this experience did for your churchgoing. Write about what you felt when you confronted the Black Madonna, alone in the woods.

Look now at a travel essay written by Emily Hiestand, excerpted from her book *The Very Rich Hours: Travels in Orkney, Belize, the Everglades, and Greece,* and reprinted in *A Woman's Path,* a collection of travel writing published by Travelers' Tales.

"Renewing the Sun"

Near dusk one night on Lésvos I am heading back to Afrodite's Rooms-to-Let through a small woods. Rounding a bend in the path, I come upon a group of women and children lighting three large brush bonfires on a scruff of beach at the outer edge of the village. As the women touch matches to the three piles of brush, the sun is just setting, and for half an hour—until the bonfires somewhat burn down—four orange-red shapes flare against the evening sky. As the sun slips into the sea and the flames diminish, the women and their children turn into silhouettes against the sky and sea. One skinny boy, about nine, suddenly bolts from the cluster and leaps over all the fires, one after another, whooping. His small, wiry boy-body, at apogee over the low flames, looks like a twisting shape the fire has thrown up. Now a girl runs forward and jumps over the fires, and then all the children do, sometimes several times, like kids shooting down slides then running around to do it again. The mothers stand talking along the seawall, their plump bodies, black skirts, and olive skins glowing in the heat. When the fires burn still lower, the children gather stones from the beach and begin hurling them into the embers. It is the twenty-first of June,

Saint John's Eve on the Christian calendar, a quasi-advent that foreshadows the winter arrival of the Savior. And on the pagan calendar tonight is the summer solstice, one of the two great turning points in the year. These hours exactly mark the time that shorter, colder days begin. In the old culture, tonight was the night of bonfires, lit all over Europe to signal, and perhaps ritually renew, the sun's waning energy.

Along the wall, one of the mothers recognizes me from the English lessons; she waves and I join her near the fires, which are still giving off a great wall of heat. She says that the girls and boys are jumping over the fires so that they will be fertile, and she encourages me to jump too. The children are excited that an adult might join them. The fires are mostly crackling-hot stones by now, with only low flames and rogue licks leaping up; still there is a moment of thrilled fear, sailing over the heat. Afterward, a boy named Alekos gives me two stones and tells me to throw them in the fire. When I do, he shrieks the Greek child's unparalleled shriek. The matronly women (who are probably ten years younger than I) giggle and look pleased with themselves. We stay until the stones grow cold and the light fails, and the women, who leapt over fires themselves not so long ago, round up their happy, spent children and go home. Unaware of their beauty, the uncountable leaves of the surrounding olive trees darken into the concentrate of all color.

Consider first the three elements of travel writing.

It is personal: Hiestand's experience. The reader feels that she knows the writer and shares her emotions, even the moment of thrilled fear. It is imaginative: there is the story of an American discovering a pagan ritual on a Greek island and entering into it, jumping over the crackling fires. And it is informative, with mythic details of the pagan celebration on the summer solstice, the night of bonfires lit to renew the sun's waning energy.

Now look at how the essay follows Zinnser's suggested unities for travel writing. The essay is written in one voice, first person, as Hiestand relates her experience. It's in one tense, the present, with the lovely closing in the present as the leaves "darken, into the concentrate of all color." Throughout the essay, there is the same mood of remembrance. Hiestand is remembering how she was enticed to participate in the pagan ritual. There is just one subject—the pagan ritual—and one thought—the importance of the ritual for the Greek inhabitants, the writer, and the reader. Heistand takes the reader to an unfamiliar place and reveals its essence.

TIPS FOR WRITING TRAVEL ESSAYS

Before you start to write your own travel essay, here is a list of tips.

— Start with something that is easily accessible.
— Take copious notes and record conversations. Immerse yourself in each place.
— Write about a place that became important to you.
— Craft carefully the opening and the ending.
— Include your own emotions and reactions.
— Focus on small, relevant details.
— Think visually; see the place.
— Include specifics—accuracy is vital.
— Leave the reader with an impression, a thought.

Remember, you are taking the reader to a new place. It is the intensity of your emotions that counts. We touch here upon "armchair traveling." Most readers will not be able to follow in your footsteps. But you can bring the experience so close to them that they will feel they have been there.

WRITING THE TRAVEL ESSAY

Keeping in mind the four steps of writing a personal essay, we will work here with the first two steps, as we did with the opinion essay.

First, choose and tell. What travel experience calls out to you? Be quiet for a moment and go within. What travel story wishes to be shared? Hold it in your imagination. Focus and frame. Don't start too early. Don't add too many details. This is your first draft. Afterward you can add more information. You are not crafting, you are free-writing.

✎ Exercise: Write a first draft of your travel essay. Ten
    minutes.

Now show (dramatize). Think about the elements of story. Think about the descriptive details, a narrative tug. What will keep your reader interested? Think back to Hiestand's essay above: the skinny boy, the mothers in black, the olive skins. The author's ambivalence about remembering (the emotions, the nostalgia, the tension). Work on dramatizing.

✎ Exercise: Work on a second draft, with a narrative tug.
    Fifteen minutes. As always, give your work a title.

You have now the beginnings of both an op-ed essay and a travel essay. You may work at your own rhythm for the third step, polishing the essay with elements of poetry. As you do this, you are deepening and highlighting its meaning. Then follows the fourth step, putting it aside for a while before rewriting.

Again, here are a few suggestions for when you feel your essay is ready to submit. Read several travel magazines. Then select three or four publications that seem suitable for your work. Read past issues of these publications. Get a feel for the style and the editorial requirements. Is this where you want your essay to be printed? And always remember that an essay is inspired, not assigned. It comes from within. For further tips on submission and publication, please see the last pages of Lesson Eleven.

Just like op-eds, travel essays reach very large audiences. Give your essay the best of your skills. Take the reader to a new place with a new light.

✎ There are four exercises in this lesson: two for writing opinion essays (the first draft, and the second draft working with the elements of story), and two for travel essays (two drafts as well). You may work on them as indicated within the lesson, or you may spend more time on each one, taking one week for each. Following these four exercises I suggest that you continue on your own to work on the third step (working with elements of poetry) and then the fourth (gestation!), to finish both your essays.

Short Stories
and the Short-Short

In lessons two and three, you moved forward from the foundation of journaling to writing essays. Here you will move to writing short stories. Your journals are seedbeds for both nonfiction and fiction. Story means narrative, and it is found in all forms of writing. Writer and instructor Eunice Scarfe writes, "The seed of story is found in every genre, told or written, imagined or remembered. If we have lived, we each have a story; if we can tell it, we can write it. Story has the power to redeem, restore and renew—and bind us together." This is story. You will work with story throughout the year. In this lesson you will work with the form of the short story and the short-short.

I turn to the short story with a certain optimism, believing along with Vince Passaro that there is a quiet renaissance of American short fiction. In his essay, "Unlikely Stories," Passaro highlighted the growing vitality of the contemporary short story

at the turn of the century. In spite of the waning of story collections and magazine outlets, compared to the Hemingway and
Fitzgerald period of the 1930s, *The New Yorker* period of the
1950s, the minimalist period of the 1980s, short fiction in the first
decade of this century is expansive, innovative, refined, and rich.

The closest we can come to defining the short story is that in
every story something happens to someone. A character is
struggling for a goal—the more noble the goal, the more important the story. A character is moved, no matter how slightly. In
this chapter we will look at the structure of the short story, its
different elements, its points of view. But we will keep in mind
that a short story is more than its parts. In *The Art of Fiction*,
John Gardner writes, "Fiction does its work by creating a vivid
and continuous dream in the reader's mind." The story, be it
short or book-length, creates a dream in the reader's mind.

It is here that the short story form appeals to almost all
writers. The challenge of inventing a dream world is alluring.
How can a vivid and continuous dream be created in the reader's
mind? How can characters come alive in a fictional landscape?
How can this be done in a short story?

INTRODUCTION TO THE SHORT STORY

When we think short story, we think character and action. Like
the subject and verb in a sentence, both are necessary in a story.
Character without action means no story. And action without
character means no transformation. John Updike wants a story
to startle and engage him within the opening few sentences, to
widen or deepen in the middle, and to give him a sense of
accomplished statement at the end.

As you practice writing the short story, you can learn from

books like John Gardner's *The Art of Fiction,* Rust Hills' *Writing in General and the Short Story in Particular,* A.B. Guthrie's *A Field Guide to Writing Fiction,* and Anne Lamott's *Bird by Bird.* You'll learn still more from reading short stories. Study Anton Chekhov, James Joyce, Flannery O'Connor, Ernest Hemingway, Alice Munro, and Lorrie Moore. Read anthologies of the best short stories and literary magazines: *The New Yorker, Ploughshares,* and *Granta* among others. Many are available either in print or online. Discover your favorite short story writers and read all that they have written. Remember that you come into this writing world on the shoulders of all those who have preceded you. Think about this, and read. Do not worry about copying. It is in reading and writing that you will find your own voice.

When I began to study the short story, I read all of Hemingway's stories and all of Flannery O'Connor's. They were my teachers. I took each story apart, trying to understand how it worked. I also read O'Connor's *Mystery and Manners: Occasional Prose,* containing essays on her peacocks but also on the nature of fiction and on writing short stories. O'Connor's title refers to her belief that through the canny—the senses—we discover the uncanny—the meaning. Through manners, we discover mystery. She writes that the short story writer can't say anything meaningful about the mystery of a personality unless the personality is situated in a believable social context.

Writers are readers. Who are your favorite short story writers? Ask yourself why. Study their stories. Why are they compelling? What makes them work? How are they structured? How are the characters portrayed? What point of view is used? Is the writer's voice important? What imagery is used? Underline all the passages that capture your imagination. Your favorite writers are your best teachers.

Let's look at a few sentences from James Joyce's classic story, "The Dead," in *Dubliners*. Here are the last lines of the story, written with such poetic beauty—the rhythm of the sentences and the focused imagery—that they are a school in themselves.

From "The Dead"

It had begun to snow again. He watched sleepily the flakes, silver and dark, falling obliquely against the lamplights. . . . It was falling on every part of the dark central plain, on the treeless hills. . . . It was falling, too, upon every part of the lovely churchyard on the hill. . . . His soul swooned slowly as he heard the snow falling faintly through the universe and faintly falling, like the descent of their last end, upon all the living and the dead.

Read the last sentence again. Snow falling faintly and faintly falling upon the living and the dead. Here, Joyce effectively creates a vivid and continuous dream in the reader's mind.

EXAMPLE OF A SHORT STORY

Before we study the structure of the short story and its different elements, here is a short story that will serve as illustration. I have chosen a very short one written before short-shorts, sudden fiction, and flash fiction were defined as a sub-genre of the short story. Just as Tolstoy, Chekhov, Maupassant, and Kafka were writing very short stories, so was Grace Paley. Here is "Wants," a complete short story in less than eight hundred words, first published in 1974.

"Wants"

I saw my ex-husband in the street. I was sitting on the steps of the new library.

Hello, my life, I said. We had once been married for twenty-seven years, so I felt justified.

He said, What? What life? No life of mine.

I said, O.K. I don't argue when there's real disagreement. I got up and went into the library to see how much I owed them.

The librarian said $32 even and you've owed it for eighteen years. I didn't deny anything. Because I don't understand how time passes. I have often thought of those books. The library is only two blocks away.

My ex-husband followed me to the Books Returned desk. He interrupted the librarian, who had more to tell. In many ways, he said, as I look back, I attribute the dissolution of our marriage to the fact that you never invited the Bertrams to dinner.

That's possible, I said. But really, if you remember: first, my father was sick that Friday, then the children were born, then I had those Tuesday-night meetings, then the war began. Then we didn't seem to know them any more. But you're right. I should have had them to dinner.

I gave the librarian a check for $32. Immediately she trusted me, put my past behind her, wiped the record clean, which is just what most other municipal and/or state bureaucracies will *not* do.

I checked out the two Edith Wharton books I had just returned because I'd read them so long ago and they are more apropos now than ever. They were *The House of Mirth* and *The Children*, which is about how life in the United

States in New York changed in twenty-seven years fifty years ago.

A nice thing I do remember is breakfast, my ex-husband said. I was surprised. All we ever had was coffee. Then I remembered there was a hole in the back of the kitchen closet which opened into the apartment next door. There, they always ate sugar-cured smoked bacon. It gave us a very grand feeling about breakfast, but we never got stuffed and sluggish.

That was when we were poor, I said.

When were we ever rich? he asked.

Oh, as time went on, as our responsibilities increased, we didn't go in need. You took adequate financial care, I reminded him. The children went to camp four weeks a year and in decent ponchos with sleeping bags and boots, just like everyone else. They looked very nice. Our place was warm in winter, and we had nice red pillows and things.

I wanted a sailboat, he said. But you didn't want anything.

Don't be bitter, I said. It's never too late.

No, he said with a great deal of bitterness. I may get a sailboat. As a matter of fact I have money down on an eighteen-foot two-rigger. I'm doing well this year and can look forward to better. But as for you, it's too late. You'll always want nothing.

He had had a habit throughout the twenty-seven years of making a narrow remark which, like a plumber's snake, could work its way through the ear down the throat, halfway to my heart. He would then disappear, leaving me choking with equipment. What I mean is, I sat down on the library steps and he went away.

I looked through *The House of Mirth,* but lost interest. I felt extremely accused. Now, it's true, I'm short of requests and absolute requirements. But I do want *something.*

I want for instance to be a different person. I want to be the woman who brings these two books back in two weeks. I want to be the effective citizen who changes the school system and addresses the Board of Estimate on the troubles of this dear urban center.

I *had* promised my children to end the war before they grew up.

I wanted to have been married forever to one person, my ex-husband or my present one. Either has enough character for a whole life, which as it turns out is really not such a long time. You couldn't exhaust either man's qualities or get under the rock of his reasons in one short life.

Just this morning I looked out the window to watch the street for a while and saw that the little sycamores the city had dreamily planted a couple of years before the kids were born had come that day to the prime of their lives.

Well! I decided to bring those two books back to the library. Which proves that when a person or an event comes along to jolt or appraise me I *can* take some appropriate action, although I am better known for my hospitable remarks.

Again, the author has created a vivid and continuous dream in the reader's mind. You want to sit down on the library steps with her. I will use this story to illustrate the structure of the short story, its different elements and point of view.

THE STRUCTURE OF THE SHORT STORY

The basic structure of the short story is three parts: beginning (the desire), middle (the struggle), end (the conclusion). In theory, these three parts form one, and a short story should be as whole as possible.

— Beginning: There is an initiatory incident in which the protagonist confronts a problem that creates a desire or need (the goal).
— Middle: The protagonist struggles to fulfill his or her desire. There are increasing complications (crises) until the climax, also referred to as the turning point.
— Ending: There is an "epiphany" (James Joyce's word, a manifestation of the "whatness" of the character or situation). The protagonist is moved. There is some sort of fulfillment, dénouement (a common writing term from French that means the "unknotting"),resolution.

If you look at the example "Wants," you see the beginning, where the protagonist is sitting on the library steps and sees her ex-husband. She wants to remember the good parts of their marriage, to reconnect in a way. This is the desire. The middle part is the dialogue with her husband and his reasons for why the marriage was dissolved—her failure to invite the Bertrams. There is a soft rise as he remembers their breakfasts. This takes her to the hole in the kitchen closet and a comparison with her neighbors: "that was when we were poor." And they arrive at the reason for their separation, their different wants. The husband wanted a sailboat. Small crises lead to the climax where he confronts her—"You'll always want nothing." And the ending: she sits back down on the library steps as he walks away. The short encounter reveals—to the narrator and to the reader—that she accepts her life as it is and is happy to see that sycamores planted before her children were born are now in their prime. All three parts are there.

As Updike wants from a short story, the reader is immediately engaged by the first sentence, the story widens in the middle, and there is completion at the end. The reader has a warm spot in his heart for the narrator.

THE DIFFERENT ELEMENTS OF THE SHORT STORY

A second consideration in studying the short story concerns its various elements. The successful contemporary short story demonstrates a harmonious relationship among all its elements: characters, plot, setting, theme, dialogue, imagery, style, point of view, and voice (the writer's vision and morality). All of these elements are interwoven—with economy—into a whole, with each element contributing to the success of the story. And this success depends upon the human significance of the story.

"Wants" shows you how Grace Paley treats these different elements:

— Characters: Both the wife and the ex-husband come alive, and the reader enters into the mind of the wife and feels her longings, her wishes, and her "wants."
— Plot: The wife is jolted by the unexpected visit of her ex-husband, remembers their years together, identifies her heartbreak, and then moves forward.
— Setting: The library steps—those three words are sufficient to create a sense of place.

— Theme: The importance of being real to oneself, of
   living each day as best as one can.
— Dialogue: Throughout the first two-thirds of the story,
   there is continual direct dialogue, without quotes but
   very clearly understood. The melding of dialogue and
   memories makes the scene very intimate. "A nice thing
   I do remember is breakfast, my ex-husband said. I was
   surprised. All we ever had was coffee. Then I remembered there was a hole in the back of the kitchen closet
   which opened into the apartment next door . . . " The
   reader moves from dialogue to memory and to intimacy.
— Imagery: From the library steps to the titles of the two
   books to the hole in the closet, the story is filled with
   images that take on meaning, as do the sycamore trees
   now in their prime. Finally, there is the invasive image
   comparing the husband's narrow remarks to a
   plumber's snake reaching halfway to the wife's heart.
   The image becomes metaphor, leaving her "choking
   with equipment."
— Style: Paley's style is recognizable, low-key, familiar,
   ironic, and compassionate.
— Point of view: It is first person, taking the reader right
   into the protagonist's mind.
— Voice: Paley's voice reflects her vision of how a marriage should be, of how to be a good citizen. Because of
   the voice, the reader comes away liking the wife (and
   the author).

All the different elements of the short story—including the
added element of ironic humor—are knit together in such a way

that the story feels complete. It is a whole. And it is successful, deeply so, because it treats human love and marriage. The reader can see him/herself in the story. The very mundane details sound familiar—the library books to return, the sugar-cured smoked bacon, the sycamores that the city had planted on the street. These are the canny details that Flannery O'Connor says are necessary in order to give the reader a sense of the uncanny, of the utter faithfulness of the narrator and of the mystery of human relations.

POINT OF VIEW

A third consideration in dealing with the short story is the point of view. First there is the choice of which character will get the point of view. Whose story is it? Another way of asking is, who is the moved character? Usually this choice is part of the author's original concept. This question is crucial to the story's success. Too often, the writer is not certain whose story she is writing. In "Wants," it is the wife's story, the wife who is moved and who therefore gets the point of view. It would be a completely different story if written from the ex-husband's point of view.

Next, should the story be written in first, second, or third person? Here is a short review of the different options:

— First person: The author stays in one character's head and writes as "I," usually appearing as if she were the character. This is clearly done in Paley's story.
— Second person: This is rarely used. I have included one story written in the second person in Lesson Seven, "Little Red Returns." The protagonist is "you."
— Third person: There are different third person voices:

- Subjective: The author stays in one person's mind and writes as "he" or "she." This allows for more distance between the author and the character than does first person. Flannery O'Connor's stories are third person subjective. So is the short-short "Carried Away" by Kevin Wilson (the next example below).
- Objective: the author stays out of the person's mind and writes as "he" or "she." Hemingway's stories are third person objective (see an example in Lesson Six).
- Omniscient: Here the writer dips into the minds of any of the characters. It is the writer playing God, seeing into everyone's hearts. This was the rule for centuries (examples are Leo Tolstoy and Henry Fielding). Then perhaps questioning God and Truth, writers looked for ways to avoid the omniscient point of view (such as Henry James and Joseph Conrad). Today, with less metaphysical questioning, authors are again using it (Joyce Carol Oates and William Gass are examples).
- Multiple: Rather than "playing God," the author skips from the point of view of one character to another, allowing the reader to know what each one feels and thinks. We see this in the short-short "Gifts" by Janet E. Gardner (last example below) where in very few words we have three different points of view.

Try writing the opening—just one paragraph—of a short story. Look for an imagined or remembered character and place him or her in an incident that calls for an action. For example, imagine a parent whose teenage son or daughter comes home late, or remember when this happened to you. Tell the parent's story. Or imagine it from the teenager's point of view and tell the teenager's story. Take a moment, close your eyes, and let the character come to you. When you have your character, think about him for a moment, picture him in you mind. If you are in a workshop environment, this is a good place to stop and share your story and character with another writer.

Then ask yourself in what person you wish to tell the character's story. Do you wish to write in first person (using the pronoun "I") or third person (using the pronoun "she" or "he")? Which seems more natural for this particular story? As you start to write, try to introduce both the character and the incident in one paragraph. Do not rush. Write a single paragraph and take your time.

✎ Exercise: Write the opening of a short story in first or
　　third person. Ten minutes.

Stretch for a moment and then write the same opening in the other person. Take a few minutes to imagine the story in the other person. The story is happening to the same character, but you will write it in a different person. You cannot simply change the pronouns; the story will change according to the point of view. Again, try just one paragraph.

✎ Exercise: Write the same opening in a different person.
　　Take ten minutes.

Now reread both exercises. Which one feels more natural? This will be the opening to your short story.

INTRODUCTION TO THE SHORT-SHORT

Back in the 1980s when sudden fiction—stories generally under two thousand words—was beginning to appear in literary magazines and in books from small presses, short-shorts were called tiny kingdoms. They present a whole world in a few pages. And in their brevity, they have an intensity of penetration into human life that is very different from the longer short story.

The first anthology of American short-shorts, *Sudden Fiction,* was edited by Robert Shapard and James Thomas in 1986. Due to its immense success, the editors published a second volume, *Sudden Fiction International,* this time including some of the best short-shorts that had been translated into English from other languages. Thomas then explored a still shorter form (under 750 words) with *Flash Fiction.* And in 1996 it was time for Shapard and Thomas to edit a third collection, *Sudden Fiction (Continued).* Such is their popularity that their fourth collection, *New Sudden Fiction: Short-Short Stories from America and Beyond,* was published in 2007, with sixty short-shorts of less than two thousand words.

Each new anthology is a testament to the vitality of the short-short that continues to be published in growing numbers, in literary magazines, small press books, and outside the traditional literary establishment—in daily newspapers and pamphlets, blogs, and website letters. Attesting to the form's popularity are multiple short-short contests in several literary reviews—*The Southeast Review, The Indiana Review, The Mid-American Review*—as well as in *Writers' Digest.*

THE APPEAL OF THE SHORT-SHORT

In addressing the short-short's popularity, Charles Baxter wrote in his introduction to *Sudden Fiction International* that he suspected these stories appealed to the reader because of their various thresholds: between poetry and fiction, between the story and the sketch, between the personal and the crowd. This multi-faceted shape of the short-short is one of its most important attractions. A second and important reason for their appeal is their very suddenness. As the editors point out in the introduction to *Sudden Fiction (Continued),* the short-short is suddenly just there. And so the word sudden, from the Latin *subire* (to steal upon, unforeseen, swift) seemed to them the absolutely appropriate name for the form.

I would like to underline another reason for their attraction, one that goes back to tiny kingdoms. Short-shorts are little islands in the middle of the increasing noise of our contemporary world, places where we can catch our breath. Technology, television, and the Internet have brought the world closer to us. We know what is happening elsewhere—and we know it now. There results an almost staggering inflow of information, and our living space is right up close. A short-short seems the right size to let us take a break.

You will read below two short-shorts to see their appeal for yourself, to see how suddenly the story is there, a tiny kingdom all by itself. But first a quick definition of the short-short: it contains all the elements of the short story plus the element of surprise. Everything depends upon its intensity—one flash of insight, one stroke of invention. Its shape is protean. Generally, short-shorts are between eight hundred and two thousand words, while flash fiction is generally under eight hundred words. Otherwise, short-shorts and flash fiction belong to the same family: short sudden fiction.

HOW THE SHORT-SHORT WORKS

First, in general, the story has to do with a sudden crisis. The situation is there first, and the character does not act so much as react. The story is too short to have room for a long buildup to the character. This often makes the situation larger than the character. Stress is applied, and the character reacts. Out of this sudden crisis comes an unexpected moment of revelation.

Second, the short-short falls somewhere between poetry and fiction. Attention is given to the poetic elements of imagery (images becoming metaphors to carry the meaning of the story), rhythm and sound (sentences with stressed and unstressed syllables, a cadence of beats, repetition of sounds and of words), and compression (a whole story compressed, distilled, into a few paragraphs). At the same time attention is given to the narrative elements: descriptive details, dialogue, tension, plotting (a rise and a fall), and some sort of resolution.

Third, short-shorts are usually open-ended, finishing with a suggestion rather than an explicit conclusion. The truth of the story is allowed to stand without explanation, almost in contradiction. A moment in time that is revealed. There is no heavy conclusion to a moment in time; there is instead suspension and a widening that stays with the reader.

Here is Kevin Wilson's short-short, "Carried Away," published in the magazine *Quick Fiction,* issue four, 2003. This journal has been around since 2001, publishing stories under five hundred words each spring and fall.

"Carried Away"

Benny was walking his dog when the hawk came and took it away. Or maybe it was a falcon. It was a very large bird, whatever it was. And now it had his dog.

"Hey," Benny said when the bird swept down and plucked the little dog from the sidewalk. The dog was too confused to even bark. "Hey," he said again. The hawk just kept flying, higher and higher. "Hey," he said one more time even though he knew that saying it again wasn't going to do anything.

He had begged his parents for over a year to get this dog. His father did not think he was responsible enough. "You're eleven years old," his father told him. "Mom still has to write your name in your underwear." Still, he was persistent, ceaseless, unwavering. He talked about dogs all the time. Pasted pictures all over his wall. Barked in his sleep.

So they gave him this little dog. It was purebred, papered, the best thing Benny had ever seen. He called it Chin-Chin, and he agreed to every rule his parents made up. He would feed it, clean up after it, walk it every day. "This is it, Benny," his father said. "You got your little dog, so I don't want to hear about any other things you want. No unicycles, no karate lessons, no anything." It was fine with Benny. He just wanted this dog.

Now Benny watched Chin-Chin getting further and further away from him. The leash still hung from the dog's neck. It reminded Benny of the time he'd lost his grip on a kite at the park and it had floated away. Oh, his dad was upset about that. He felt so stupid that he hadn't held onto the leash. The dog was his responsibility.

There were so many things that he had worried about. Cars. Other, bigger dogs. Other, bigger kids. His father. He had never, even in his worst nightmares, imagined that a giant, winged thing would carry his dog away from him.

The hawk and the dog were gone now, out of sight. Benny still couldn't move. He was crying; he could feel the tears streaking his face. The world was mean and unfair in the strangest ways.

He knew that his father would not get him another dog. He now realized that his father might not even believe his story about the hawk. He did not want to go home. He thought about the place that the hawk was taking his dog, somewhere far, far from this spot on the sidewalk, and he wished more than anything that he could go there with them.

In this short-short, there is a sudden crisis. Benny is walking his dog when a hawk carries Chin-Chin away. The situation is there. Benny does not make the crisis appear. It comes out of the sky. What can he do? Only remember how he loved the dog, how he got the dog, how he promised to do everything for the dog, how his father won't believe him, how he is now afraid to go home. The story proceeds all in flashback, in remembering.

The story is carefully crafted with poetic details. Benny's "Hey" repeated three times—"Hey" Benny said, "Hey," he said again, "Hey," he said one more time—would be just as effective in a poem as it is in this short-short. The image of the dog flying away with the leash still hanging down reminding Benny of when he'd lost his grip on a kite is central to the story. The writer turns the image of the kite disappearing into a metaphor for Benny's childhood. For the dream that Benny was holding on to as a child.

The story is a whole, using narrative details of description, plotting, dialogue, and resolution. The rise and fall are in flashbacks: when he receives the dog, all his promises to his father, all the things he will do for the dog, all his fears. But never had he feared that a very large bird would drop out of the sky to pluck Chin-Chin away, farther and farther away.

And last there is the widening of the conclusion, the suspended moment: Benny's desire to disappear with his dog. A moment of suspension, yes, as the winged thing carries his dog away from him and as Benny wishes to follow them. You, the reader, also remember moments when your childhood dreams disappeared.

Here is a still-shorter flash fiction (just under two hundred words), "Gifts," by Janet E. Gardner, published in *Vestal Review,* a print and online magazine that is devoted to flash fiction.

"Gifts"

That Christmas, just before she went into the hospital, Joanie gave everyone kaleidoscopes. Pale, smooth wooden ones for her mother and sister; a sleek, pen-sized model in burnished steel for Helen; brightly-colored plastic ones for all the children she knew. And for Stefan—the most extravagant gift she had ever given—a four-hundred-dollar brass instrument from Switzerland, with precision optics and semi-precious stone fragments suspended in a think liquid that held their refracted images in slow flux.

"We should have known," Helen would say later. "The kaleidoscopes were a sign." A sign, she meant, of the troubled mind that would wake Joanie up one bright dawn and make her walk without hesitation out of the hospital and into the river, smiling and blinking at the scatterings of sunlight on the surface of the icy January water as it closed around her.

That afternoon, chastened by his own lack of surprise or grief, Stefan would take his kaleidoscope from its stand on the mantle. It would be the first time he had touched it since Christmas, and now he would gaze through if for most of an hour at a vivid, slow-moving, shattered world.

Each of the characters in this story reacts to a sudden crisis. Joanie reacts to her hospitalization by giving kaleidoscopes: an image that takes on symbolic meaning, revealing that beneath her troubled mind there is a pattern of sanity. She will leave her family and friends with a symbol of the shattered world that does her in. Helen reacts, realizing too late why Joanie had chosen kaleidoscopes to give as gifts. And Stefan reacts last, gazing for most of an hour at a shattered world—now his shattered world. As does the reader.

Again, the writer has paid attention to the elements of poetry. "Pale, smooth wooden ones for her mother and sister . . ." As you read this, you slow down, each word wants to be pronounced, each syllable stressed. The same for "a sleek pen-sized model in burnished steel for Helen." And then the kaleidoscope with semi-precious fragments "suspended in a thick liquid that held their refracted images in slow flux." The kaleidoscope becomes a metaphor for the world around Joanie, the protagonist, a world that will destroy her, "smiling and blinking at the scatterings of sunlight on the surface of the icy January water." The repetitions of the s's slide over the surface of the icy water.

At the same time the writer has paid attention to the narrative details. In giving kaleidoscopes to her friends, Joanie forewarns both them and the reader that her life will soon be shattered. The details of each kaleidoscope are effectively rendered to characterize each friend. Dialogue adds to the narration as it moves to Helen's new awareness, as does the long act of gazing increase Stephen's awareness.

The open ending shows Stefan at last confronting the vivid, slow moving, shattered world of the kaleidoscope. Confronting his own shattered world. As reader you do not know his reaction. Instead you are suspended in time, confronting your own shattered world.

Look also at the title. "Gifts." A title that magnifies the tragedy of the story. Pay attention to titles. When well chosen, they expand the story.

WRITING THE SHORT-SHORT

Now it's your turn to write a short-short, or better a flash fiction—fewer words (under five hundred) and more time to compress—in two guided exercises. Here are a few guidelines.

— Either go back to the character that you wrote about in the first exercise, or find a different imagined or remembered character.

— Place the character in an existing situation that creates a need or desire. Remember that the opening situation is central to a short-short. The suddenness concerns the character's reaction to this opening situation. Before beginning, go within. Let the story of the character and the situation surface in your imagination.

— Once you have the story (remembered or imagined), picture the character and decide in which person you will write: in first person (like Grace Paley's "Needs") or in third person (like Janet Gardner's "Gifts" or Kevin Wilson's "Carried Away").

— Introduce the character and the situation in one or two lines. Then move to the middle part, writing the rise and fall of the situation—here is your story. Don't impose a conclusion; let yourself be surprised. Write slowly.

✎ Exercise: Start to write a short-short. Fifteen minutes.

After fifteen minutes stop and see where you are. Have you shown the opening situation and character? Have you written the middle, the development of the story, the complication? Are you ready to find the way to your open ending? Has your character moved? If you are working with a group of writers, read your story to the person next to you. If you are alone, read it aloud. Listen to your words. Make them flow. Look at the imagery. Go back now for another fifteen minutes.

✎ Exercise: Continue; let the ending linger. Fifteen minutes. Remember to name your short-short.

If I had to find one word for the short-short, for this tiny kingdom, I would settle for "luminous." May you enjoy making your short-shorts luminous!

✎ In this lesson, you have two short exercises (the opening of a short story, and the same opening in a different point of view) of ten minutes each, and then two longer exercises (starting a short-short, and then working through to an open ending) of fifteen minutes each. If you follow this timing, you can do the lesson in one setting. Or, as is the case with every lesson, you can spread the exercises out over the course of a month, one week for each.

Dreams and Writing

Along the way of writing, you have crafted journals, personal essays, opinion and travel essays, short stories, short-shorts. So many bursts of writing, stories brought forth as you harvest your journals. During the first lesson, you wrote to the core, following May Sarton's example in *Journal of a Solitude*—writing down to the rocky depths, to the matrix, there where the fossil, gem, or crystal is embedded. Lesson Five asks you to use your dreams to tap still deeper into this creative source within. In the hands of writers, dreams are powerful tools.

In *Our Dreaming Mind,* Robert Van De Castle writes that crossing the threshold from the waking state to the dreaming state enriches our imagery and empowers our creativity. When you move from your daytime life to your nighttime dreams, you move from the visible to the invisible. Your dreams open the way to a whole new inner world. C.G. Jung defines the dream as the little hidden door in the innermost recesses of the soul. Before you can write from your dreams, you need to remember them and work with them. They will then lead you to this inner world.

THE HISTORY OF DREAMS

From the dawn of history, humankind has listened to dreams as messages from the gods. The earliest recorded dreams date back to 3200 B.C.E. in ancient Mesopotamia, when the Sumerians chronicled them in pictographs. In 3000 B.C.E. in Egypt, there were dream temples in Memphis devoted to the worship of Serapis, the god of dreams. The Hebrews turned to their dreams to listen to Yahweh. The Old Testament is filled with dreams. Jacob dreamed of a ladder to the heavens with angels ascending and descending, and Yahweh standing over him (Genesis 28:12).

In the fifth century BCE the Greeks built dream temples. The most famous was at Epidaurus, where people came for the services of Aesclepius, the legendary healer. The temple was round with a well in the center in which there were snakes—symbols of transformation, as they shed their skins and grow new ones. Every night when the lamps were extinguished, the priests and priestesses would chant, "Sleep now, dream now, dream the dream of the Healing God, sleep now, dream now." In the morning dream doctors listened and healed. I use this same litany often as I go to sleep at night, as a way to open myself to the world of dreams.

At about the same time in China, the Taoist Chuang-tzu dreamed his famous butterfly dream, where upon waking he no longer knew if he were the butterfly dreaming he was a man, or if he were the man dreaming he was a butterfly. Meanwhile in

India, Maya, Buddha's mother, dreamed the conception of her son as she was transported into the sky.

A thousand years later in 594 of our era, Muhammed received his divine mission in a dream and passed along to his disciples his daily practice of listening to dreams. In the Western world, Hildegard of Bingen, the twelfth-century Benedictine mystic, musician, and healer, received her wisdom through visions, dreaming of the spheres of the universe and of all beings celebrating the creation. But toward the end of the Middle Ages, dreams were relegated to the netherworld and entered the domain of demons and devils. The Catholic Church strongly resisted the world of dreams. So great was the mistrust of them that Martin Luther prayed to have no recollection of his dreams. Centuries passed, and the Enlightenment liberated dreams from the devil and the inquisitors. Philosophers and scientists studied them with a rational mind. In the nineteenth century, the Romantic School looked into the significance of dreams, prefiguring Freud and Jung.

Our modern understanding of dreams was ushered in with Freud's *The Interpretation of Dreams* in 1900, which hails dreams as the "royal road to the unconscious." Freud's colleague C.G. Jung delved still deeper into the unconscious to include not only the personal unconscious, but also the collective unconscious—our common heritage of myths, folklore, and legends.

WRITING FROM DREAMS

When we dream we are transported into a different world: the world of the unconscious where the language is imagery, where our senses are enlivened and our imagination enriched. Michael

Ondaatje opens his book *Running in the Family* with: "What began it all was the bright bone of a dream I could hardly hold onto. I was sleeping at a friend's house. I saw my father, chaotic, surrounded by dogs, all of them were screaming and barking into the tropical landscape. The noises woke me. I sat up on the uncomfortable sofa and I was in a jungle, hot, sweating. . . . It was a new winter and I was already dreaming of Asia." So begins—with a dream—his evocative journal of his journey back to his magical childhood in Sri Lanka.

In *Writers Dreaming* by Naomi Epel, William Styron explains "The whole concept of *Sophie's Choice* was the result if not of a dream, of a kind of waking vision which occurred when I woke up with this lingering vision . . . a merging from the dream to a conscious vision and memory of this girl named Sophie. And it was powerful because I lay there in bed with the abrupt knowledge that I was going to deal with this as a work of fiction. . . . That very morning I walked over to my studio and wrote down the first words just as they are in the book."

Maya Angelou, also interviewed in *Writers Dreaming,* states "Dreams can tell people all sorts of things, can work out problems. Especially for writing . . . The brain says, 'Okay, you go to sleep, I'll take care of it.' The dream allows the person to do things, to think things, to go places and be acted upon. The person in real time would never do these things. . . . There's a phrase in West Africa called 'deep talk', when an older person will often use a parable, an axiom, and then add, 'Take that as deep talk.' Meaning . . . you can continue to go down deeper and deeper. Dreams may be deep talk."

And so it was for my memoir, *Looking for Gold*. Once the book and most of its chapters came to me in a dream at a writers' conference in New York, I never doubted that I should write it. My dream opened the door—a little crack—to something deep within me, not only to my own unconscious but to a deeper collective unconscious. I worked with myths and legends from centuries back, from different cultures, each time enriching my experience, enriching my writing.

If you slow down and think back to your dreams, which one is now calling for your attention? First close your eyes and let your mind be still for a moment. What dream wishes to be remembered? A dream you had recently? One from a long time ago? Write it as you remember it. Take your time and let the dream lead your hand.

✎ Exercise: Write down a dream. Ten minutes.

WORKING WITH A DREAM

Maya Angelou writes about a recurring dream of a very tall building that is in the process of being built, with scaffolds and steps. She is climbing it, from the inside, with alacrity and joy. She delights in the dream because it means that her work is going well or will go well. I also have a recurring dream, one of a young child, often a baby, that I have been neglecting and who needs attention. In it I go back to the child to take care of her. She smiles at me and finds new life. When I wake and write it down, I am encouraged. The child is my creative self. I realize that yes, I have been forgetting my own creativity, my inner child, but that now I am paying attention. The child is still there, still alive.

To work with a dream, the first step is to write it down. Keep a pencil and paper by the bedside so that even in the middle of the night you can write down a few words. Otherwise, the dream will go back to the unconscious side and you will forget it. Second, note your feelings about the dream. Feelings about dreams attract other feelings and memories. Angelou's delight in climbing the steps inside the building reminds her that she has done this before, that she will succeed. My feelings of relief at dreaming once again of a young child wash over me with fresh creativity. Third, make associations. What is the dream addressing in your life, now or in the past?

In the next step, in Jungian thinking, you amplify the dream image. This is where you dip into the collective unconscious— the treasure chest of myths, fairy tales, legends, and art—and follow your image into a deeper world. You find a myth, fairy tale, or legend that brings new resonance to your image, that enlarges its meaning. I return to my young child and I may remember Cinderella and what happens to her when she is no longer forgotten and mistreated. Or I may think of a myth: Demeter and her daughter Persephone, when Demeter finally finds her after Pluto has taken her to the underworld and when all of nature flourishes anew.

There is still a fifth step for working with a dream. I call this step animation. You animate the dream—you give it life. A dream is like a plant. If you pull it out of the dark, out of the earth, and expose it to too much sunlight, too much thought and interpretation, it will dry out and die. But if instead you go down into the dark and water its roots, it will continue to flower. You animate the dream by drawing it, acting it, and writing about it. This way you can go back to it months later, or even years later, and it will still be alive.

To recap, here are the suggested five steps for working with a dream.

— Remember your dream; write it down.
— What were your feelings about the dream?
— What associations can you make?
— What amplification can you find?
— What animation can you use to keep the dream alive?

Now to work with step five, to use writing as a way to animate your dream, you may return to the dream you wrote down in the first exercise. Read it slowly and find an image (remember an image is something you can draw) that resonates, that calls your attention. Circle the image. If you do not find an image in your dream, close your eyes and daydream for a few minutes. What image comes before you? Describe in writing the image (the one you have circled or the one you have just daydreamed), letting it lead you where it will.

✎ Exercise: Find an image in your dream and describe it.
   Ten minutes.

FOLLOWING THE IMAGE

Another way to keep the image alive is to draw it. Just as you drew mandalas with your images from your journal writing, so you may draw mandalas with the images from your dreams. You have found an image in your dream and you have described it. Now place your image in a mandala. You will remember from the first lesson that the word simply means circle, the symbol of wholeness. What is important in the mandala is the movement outward from the center to the world, and then the return movement inward from the world to the center.

Hildegard of Bingen, the twelfth-century Benedictine abbess, was graced from the age of eight with the gift of visions. Out of humility, she concealed her gift in silence until the age of forty-two when, while very sick, she heard a voice, "Write what you see and hear!" Hildegard started to write and draw pictures of her visions, many of which were mandalas. She drew her visions in circles, representing the cosmos, circles of water, fire, air. She recovered her health and with new strength became the teacher, healer, and prophet whom we know and celebrate today.

When I draw a mandala with an image from my dreams, it casts its light on my world, deepening my understanding of where I am in my life. I try to not think as I let my hand draw. Here is an example from one of the many dreams I have noted about forgetting a young child. First the dream: "May 16, 2004: I have been away for a while. A baby's crib is fit into place and I am taking care of a baby. She is standing in her crib. By moments it is Lucie (our youngest daughter) close to one year old. She is very dear. I realize I have not spent much time with her and I think I now will do so. She is a soft, lovely baby and seems to recognize me. I put her down to sleep, she smiles and snuggles into her bed."

I wrote the dream in my journal and later, when I went back to it, I drew a young child in a small mandala. I see her standing in the middle of the circle. She is my creative self. From this center, light radiates upward. I penciled in a diamond around her—north, south, east, west. At the top of the mandala, there is a half circle of emerging light. At the bottom there is a half circle of deepening darkness. This drawing continues to reassure me. My creative self is there, in the center, reaching outward and rising into the light.

My Creative Child, Bellevue, 2004

So now draw a mandala. Take a piece of paper—a half piece or smaller to put in your journal—and draw a circle the size that you wish. Draw another circle for the center. Place your image inside this smaller circle, or if you wish, let it circle around the center Fill in the rest of your mandala, letting your imagination play. Where is the image taking you?

✎ Exercise: Draw a mandala with your dream image. Ten minutes.

When you've finished, look at your mandala. Let your eyes be drawn to the center and then outward. And back to the center. Do this slowly. Name your mandala; give it a title. As I mentioned earlier, naming is always important. It is a creative exercise in itself. When you return to your mandala, the title speaks to you. You remember where you were at the moment you drew it and named it. Not where you were physically, in your office or a classroom, but where you were spiritually. Where you were in your soul. When seen this way mandalas become soul maps, itineraries of your spiritual journey.

LISTENING TO THE IMAGE

You have followed the image from your dream, letting it open the door to your unconscious. You have drawn it in a mandala, and now you will talk to the image. This is all part of keeping the dream alive. Jung called it active imagination. First you empty your mind of mindful thinking, then through imagining you give outer expression to an inner image. In its simplest terms, it is akin to conscious daydreaming. It is also akin to what Brenda Ueland, in *If You Want to Write,* calls "moodling." She writes that imagination needs moodling— long, inefficient, happy idling, dawdling and puttering. This quiet looking and listening will bring out ideas and feelings from deep within.

So imagine a dialogue, a conversation with your image. You have to be idle and alone, quietly looking and listening. Speak to your image. Why did it come to you today? What does it have to say to you? Write a dialogue. Start by asking a question to your image; ask it why it is here with you today. Perhaps start with "What do you want?" And listen and wait. Let the image answer you. "I want . . ." Take your time and imagine your conversation. Write the questions and answers in the form of a dialogue.

✎ Exercise: Write a dialogue with your image. Ten
   minutes.

SHAPING THE STORY OF THE IMAGE INTO WRITING

Stories from dream images find their place in all forms of writing. Here is an essay written by Robert Vivian that includes a very vivid dream. In "Light Calling to Other Light" (published in *Fourth Genre*, Spring 2000), Vivian writes about collecting scraps of light in order to deal with the darkness in the world. He puts the scraps in an imaginary bag the size of a small yard that collapses into a hand-held pouch when he goes to sleep at night. To amplify his theme, Vivian includes a dream in which he flies on the wings of a sea gull to the outer rim of light, becoming one with its translucent wings.

FROM "LIGHT CALLING TO OTHER LIGHT"

In a dream once I saw the translucent wings of a sea gull banked against the sun. It screeched out to me or to no one. And as the gull passed for that outer rim of light, I was suddenly there, too, in the bird's wings, holding the stitches [of the pouch] in place against the oncoming fire. Wheeling, circling, the sea gull was trying to show me something. . . .

For who would deny the lights of dreams? What are they if not reverberations of the sun and suns that made them? We are not what we think we are, bodies and ribs shackled to the ground. We are the sea gull's transparent wings, the prism of colors in the bird's burning feathers. . .

We are light calling for other light, and these lights come careening from all angles, we cannot stop them. And I collect these scraps of light because I'm weary and because I'm hungry. I collect them so that when it is late or the bad news keeps coming, I can put my wrists right through them to the elbow and let them hold me for a while.

Light calling to other light, splendor of the sun-blanched

stone, we close our eyes to the sun so that other, less blinding suns may enter and we can gather them and give them away when the brightness is too much.

Vivian's dream takes the reader wheeling and circling into the sky like the sea gull, along with the writer, collecting scraps of light in order to give them away. Light calling to other light, sharing the scraps, giving them away when there is too much brightness.

The dream can also be written in a journal entry. Alice Walker includes a beautiful dream in her collection of prose, *Living by the Word*. In this dream she is talking and laughing with Langston Hughes hugging and kissing "for an endless warm time." When she wakes in the rainy morning and realizes it is only a dream, she begins to cry. But the dream stays real and comforts her. There is a place where she and Langston can be together.

In the same way, dreams can be written as short stories. Brady Udall explains that his story "The Wig," published in the magazine *Story*, came from an image of a dream. He woke up one morning with the image stuck in his head: a small boy was sitting at the table wearing a wig and his father was very distraught by this. He had only to ask himself why the father was so distraught and the answer came quickly. He went to his desk and wrote down the story, with a father seeing his son in a blond wig, making the boy look very much like his mother who had recently died.

The story of a dream image can also find itself on a page of a memoir or a novel. Remember how Ondaatje started his memoir *Running in the Family* with the dream of seeing his father surrounded by dogs barking into the hot jungle night. Remember also how Styron started his novel *Sophie's Choice* with a dream image of a woman walking into a boarding house in New York City.

Or the image can be written as a poem. We will look more extensively at poetry in Lesson Eight. For now, it is good to remember that many of the same writing techniques apply to both poetry and prose. In *Writers Dreaming* Reynolds Price talks about how many of his poems are generated directly by dreams. In these instances when he wakes up, he sits down and writes the dream as a straightforward poem— "The Dream of a House," "The Dream of Food," "The Dream of Lee."

Now take your time as you start to shape the story of your image into a piece of writing. It can be a journal entry, a personal essay, a narrative, the beginning of a memoir or of a novel, a few lines of lyrical prose, or a poem about your image. Finally, do not worry about the form, just write. Let the image shape itself, like clay finds its form in the potter's hands.

✎ Exercise: Write the story of your image in whatever
    shape comes to you. Ten minutes. And find the title
    that fits.

Realize that you can continue to do this whenever you remember a dream and write it down Hold the dream in your imagination and find an image that speaks to you. Now hold the image in your imagination. Look at it. Draw the image in a mandala. Listen to the image in a dialogue. Then write its story. Let your dreams take you to deeper writing in whatever genre you are working in. Whether you're a novelist, essayist, poet, or playwright, let your dreams open the door to your more creative self.

✎ In this lesson, you have five exercises: writing a dream, describing a dream image, drawing it in a mandala, dialoguing with it, and shaping it into a piece of writing. Each exercise can be done quickly, in ten minutes. If you wish to do the exercises over a period of a month, the second and third exercises may be done together. The last exercise merits more time.

Dialogue

From the lesson about writing from dreams, we move on to a lesson devoted to craft. Writing good dialogue in whatever genre—fiction, nonfiction, poetry, or drama—may look easy, but it is a true craft that requires practice. You the writer must listen to the real voices around you and the imaginary ones inside you. You have to "wool gather," as Anne Lamott writes in *Bird by Bird*.

Good dialogue enlightens the reader. A space opens up and the reader steps onto the page, slows down, dips into the thoughts of each person speaking. Bad dialogue, on the other hand, blocks the reader. Often, the writer has simply reproduced actual speech without worrying about its rhythm and flow. How do you craft good dialogue? This lesson will examine the different elements of dialogue, looking at examples from past masters and leading you to write your own dialogue.

INTRODUCTION TO DIALOGUE

Dialogue looks simple, but it is one of the most difficult crafts for the writer to master. It seems as if all you have to do is listen to the way people talk and write it down. But dialogue is not just conversation. The word's origins show us that *dia* means between, and *logos* means word, wisdom, or reason, which point to a deeper definition: an exchange of meaningful thoughts rather than a conversation. It is good to think back to *The Dialogues* of Plato. They are dramatic sketches that Socrates' pupil Plato composed in order to preserve the ideas, interests and personality of his master.

Here is a passage from the dialogue entitled "Meno," where Socrates interrogates Meno about his slave.

FROM "MENO"

Socrates. What do you say of him, Meno? Were not all these
    answers given out of his own head?

Meno. Yes, they were all his own.

Socrates. And yet, as we were just saying, he did not know?

Meno. True.

Socrates. But still he had in him those notions of his—had
    he not?

Meno. Yes.

Socrates. . . . Now, has any one ever taught him all this? You
    must know about him, if, as you say, he was born and
    bred in your house.

Meno. And I am certain that no one ever did teach him.

Socrates. And yet he has the knowledge?

Meno. The fact, Socrates, is undeniable.

Socrates is using dialogue as a form of teaching. And the reader follows the exchange closely. You want to know what Socrates will ask next. How is it that Meno's slave has ready-made notions in his head? In this lesson Plato's example serves as a reminder that dialogue is not chatter, but rather the exchange of meaningful ideas.

DIALOGUE IN FICTION

Dialogue is one of the three building blocks of fiction. John Gardner writes in *The Art of Fiction* that every story is built of three units: a passage of description, a passage of dialogue, and an action. Description, dialogue, action. And it is the passages of dialogue that give life to the characters and to what is happening, making the story more dramatic, just as spoken dialogue does on the stage.

Hemingway a master of dialogue, wrote the short story "The Sea Change" all in dialogue, all in the third person objective point of view. The story is about a woman leaving the man she has been living with. Hemingway does not use one word too many or too few. The reader is left heartbroken for both the man and the woman. Here is the opening and the first third of the short story.

From "The Sea Change"

"All right," said the man. "What about it?"

"No," said the girl, "I can't."

"You mean you won't."

"I can't," said the girl. "That's all that I mean."

"You mean you won't."

"All right," said the girl. "You have it your own way."

"I don't have it my own way. I wish to God I did."

"You did for a long time," the girl said.

It was early, and there was no one in the café except the barman and these two who sat together at a table in the corner. It was the end of the summer and they were both tanned, so that they looked out of place in Paris. The girl wore a tweed suit, her skin was a smooth golden brown, her blond hair was cut short and grew beautifully away from her forehead. The man looked at her.

"I'll kill her," he said.

"Please don't," the girl said. She had very fine hands and the man looked at them. They were slim and brown and very beautiful.

"I will. I swear to God I will."

"It won't make you happy."

"Couldn't you have gotten into something else? Couldn't you have gotten into some other jam?"

"It seems not," the girl said. "What are you going to do about it?"

"I told you."

"No; I mean really."

"I don't know," he said. She looked at him and put out her hand.

"Poor old Phil," she said. He looked at her hands, but he did not touch her hand with his.

Through well-crafted, direct dialogue, Hemingway lets you, the reader, listen to this intimate conversation as if you are sitting at the table with the man and the woman. There is no distance. The dialogue proceeds in alternate beats, each line a beat, giving a rhythmic structure to the exchange. What is said reveals their characters, adds tension, creates the mood. As does what is not said. Does Hemingway need to identify the one pronoun, "I'll kill her"? No. Does he need to explain (tell) that the woman is leaving her husband in order to live with a woman? The reader understands. The hidden dialogue communicated through gestures and pauses sometimes speaks more loudly than the spoken dialogue. We see the man's eyes often resting on the woman's hands. We see her put out her hand. And we see him not touching it. We want him to take it but he does not. The gestures root the dialogue in the physical world, amplifying the spoken dialogue.

Look at how Hemingway identifies the speakers. "All right," said the man, "What about it?" "No," said the girl. Then the dialogue continues but without "said the man," "said the girl." There are two things to note here. First, it is better to use the verb phrase "he said" rather than something more complicated—"he pleaded" or "he exclaimed." The more complicated verb calls attention to itself and stops the flow of the dialogue. Second, once it has been established who is speaking, the dialogue can continue without repeating, "he said," "she said." The choice of the words themselves should reveal who is speaking. Each character speaks differently using a different syntax, even a different vocabulary.

Turn now to the opening scene in Tracy Chevalier's novel, *Girl with a Pearl Earring*. The first page is mostly description, with the action of the arrival of Vermeer and his wife, coming to inspect the young girl who will be their maid, carefully interwoven. The second page offers a very brief dialogue, "So this is the girl then," Vermeer's wife said abruptly. With just six words, the reader is forewarned that Vermeer's wife will be difficult. This is followed by the brilliant dialogue between Vermeer and the young girl Griet, through which the writer reveals Vermeer's fascination with Griet as she chops vegetables for the soup. In the following excerpt, it is important to appreciate the spoken words, but also the unspoken ones, the gestures, the asides, the pauses.

From *Girl with a Pearl Earring*

"What have you been doing here, Griet?" he asked.

I was surprised by the question but knew enough to hide it. "Chopping vegetables, sir. For the soup."

I always laid vegetables out in a circle, each with its own section like a slice of pie. There were five slices: red cabbage, onions, leeks, carrots and turnips. I had used a knife edge to shape each slice, and placed a carrot disc in the centre.

The man tapped his finger on the table. "Are they laid out in the order in which they will go into the soup?" he suggested, studying the circle.

"No, sir." I hesitated. I could not say why I had laid out the vegetables as I did. I simply set them as I felt they should be but I was too frightened to say so to a gentleman.

"I see you have separated the whites," he said, indicating the turnips and the onions. "And then the orange and the purple, they do not sit together. Why is that?" He picked up a shred of cabbage and a piece of carrot and shook them like dice in his hand.

I looked at my mother, who nodded slightly.

"The colors fight when they are side by side, sir."

He arched his eyebrows, as if he had not expected such a response. "And do you spend much time setting out the vegetables before you make the soup?"

"Oh no, sir," I replied, confused. I did not want him to think I was idle.

The reader is drawn into the scene. There in the kitchen, we listen to the dialogue between the domineering Vermeer and the humble yet astute Griet and are witness to the electricity between the two. In one page of dialogue, the descriptive shadings and the earnestness of the exchange set the tone of the entire novel.

The excerpt provides an excellent example of the three types of dialogue: direct, indirect, and hidden.

— Direct dialogue: Two or more characters are speaking together, directly to one another. This calls for quotation marks. "What have you been doing here, Griet?" asks the man. "Chopping vegetables, sir. For the soup." The direct exchange between Vermeer and Griet continues, interspersed with indirect and hidden dialogue.

— Indirect dialogue: Often, a character speaks to himself or tells something without specific words. This does not call for quotation marks unless the character is speaking aloud. Here is Griet saying something without words: "I was surprised by the question but knew enough to hide it." And then, "I could not say why I had laid out the vegetables as I did" —more indirect dialogue, giving the reader immediate information and intensifying the tone.

— Hidden dialogue: This includes everything else in a dialogue. The gestures, the hesitations, the repetitions, the glances, the asides, and the words not said. This is the subtext, running underneath the spoken text, often more powerful than spoken dialogue. Vermeer taps his finger on the table, he shakes the cabbage and carrot like dice, he arches his eyebrows, each gesture calling Griet's attention, as well as the reader's. He is imperious. Listen to him.

DIALOGUE IN NONFICTION

Strictly speaking, dialogue is not one of the structural units of
nonfiction, as it is of fiction. Sometimes nonfiction is discursive,
without dialogue; sometimes it is scenic, with dialogue. As I mentioned in Lesson Two, creative nonfiction was so termed by the
National Endowment for the Arts in the early 1970s because nonfiction writers were using fictional techniques to enhance their
writing. Hence the use of dialogue to make the story more dramatic. The writer of nonfiction writes dialogue as she remembers
it. She does not invent dialogues that did not happen.

Think of how dialogue is used in *Angela's Ashes* by Frank
McCourt, or *I Know Why the Caged Bird Sings* by Maya Angelou.
Both memoirs come alive through remembered short dialogues.
They move the story forward, reveal the characters, and pull the
reader into the story. The voice of the narrator is carefully
crafted with the same inflections throughout both memoirs.

Look at the following excerpt from the memoir *The Color of
Water* by James McBride. In this black man's tribute to his
white mother, McBride alternates two stories, the mother's and
the son's, as he explores the meaning of family and selfhood. In
the excerpt, McBride as a young boy is walking home with his
mother after church, trying to understand why she cries during
the service, if it is related to her being white, and if God likes
white people less than black people. Listen to how McBride uses
dialogue.

FROM CHAPTER SIX, "THE NEW TESTAMENT"

"Why do you cry in church?" I asked her one afternoon
after service.

"Because God makes me happy."

"Then why cry?"

"I'm crying 'cause I'm happy. Anything wrong with that?"

"No," I said, but there was, because happy people didn't seem to cry like she did. Mommy's tears seemed to come from somewhere else, a place far away, a place inside her that she never let any of us children visit, and even as a boy I felt there was pain behind them. I thought it was because she wanted to be black like everyone else in church, because maybe God liked black people better, and one afternoon on the way home from church I asked her whether God was black or white.

A deep sigh. "Oh boy . . . God's not black. He's not white. He's a spirit."

"Does he like black or white people better?"

"He loves all people. He's a spirit."

"What's a spirit?"

"A spirit's a spirit."

"What color is God's spirit?"

"It doesn't have a color," she said. "God is the color of water. Water doesn't have a color."

We have here a whole theology of God in a few words of direct dialogue. There is also indirect dialogue when McBride writes, "I asked her whether God was black or white," followed by the answer in direct dialogue. And there is hidden dialogue, expressed in the unwritten silences after each one of the mother's unsparing answers. And in the deep sigh. When the mother sighs, you the reader know that she understands the depth of her son's question. After the sigh, she says, "Oh boy . . . God's not black." Again, there is hidden dialogue in the ellipsis (McBride's). The mother is pausing. The reader pauses. The mother is going to try to answer honestly. And we the readers are not going to forget her answer: God is the color of water.

THE ELEMENTS OF GOOD DIALOGUE

In short, good dialogue achieves this effect by simultaneously revealing character and advancing the plot. In the excerpt from *Girl with a Pearl Earring,* this is done flawlessly, and the reader sizes up both Vermeer and the young girl, as well as their ensuing relationship. Likewise, in the lines of dialogue from *The Color of Water* the reader feels both the son's anxiety and his mother's patience, and anticipates how the young boy's growing respect for his mother will move the story forward. Third, good dialogue brings the reader into the scene, contributing to the tone of the encounter. In the opening of the story "The Sea Change," as in the two other passages of dialogue, you are present in the scene, catching all the vibrations expressed in the carefully crafted dialogue. You are moved by the intimacy of the exchange.

When you are writing, keep in mind that good dialogue has three functions:

— It reveals the characters (and because dialogue shows what happens between—*dia*—characters, it works to reveal each of the characters speaking in the dialogue).

— It advances the plot (and because dialogue is a meaningful exchange—*logos*—it moves the action forward and deepens the theme).

— It contributes to the tone (atmosphere) of the encounter (giving a sense of real time and intimacy so that the reader feels present in the scene).

As a last example, I have included a poem to show how dialogue can also be effectively used in poetry. "Coffee at the Café du Soleil," by short-story writer and poet Alistair Scott, was first published in *Offshoots V, Writing from Geneva.*

"COFFEE AT CAFÉ DU SOLEIL"

The conversation curls and coils,
steam rises from my *café crème*
rich aromatic half-heard words,
a swirl of laughter,
"Ouais, mais zut . . ."

A solitary woman sits,
nursing a drink. Her lighter twists
in ringless fingers. Two old *potes,*
with swooping hands, replay
the match that lost the Cup last night.
Their Gitanes trace soft arcs of smoke.

"Marcel!"
The waiter winds between
the tables, serving jokes and beer.
No one turns round as, in the door,
a man shakes rain-drops from his sleeve,
converses with a mobile phone.
Talks loud. Talks fast.
"Achète! Achète!
C'est le moment. . . "
His words dart. Sharp.

I drain my cup
look up to where
the rain-flecked window-pane
distorts the church clock's earnest face
and gently mocks its measured turn.

And I have time
to order coffee once again.
"Marcel!"

The dialogue in this poem takes the reader into the café to sit down at the table with the poet. Look at how it contributes to the three functions:

— Revealing character: The short snatches of words that the narrator picks up show his feelings as he sits there in the café. He latches on to half-heard words, promising stories and even half truths. Then, *"Achète! Achète! C'est le moment . . ."* He overhears something urgent—it's the right time to buy—and still he turns back to his coffee.

— Advancing the plot: The stanzas build on one another, and the spoken words lead the poem forward. The repetition of the waiter's name, shouted out above the din of the café, "Marcel!" "Marcel!" brings you into the café.

— Contributing to the tone: By including dialogue in his poem, Scott creates the atmosphere of the café scene. And he lets you the reader sense the narrator's mood.

TIPS FOR WRITING GOOD DIALOGUE

Before you start to write a dialogue, here are some practical suggestions.

— Listen to conversations around you (in the elevator, at dinners, on the bus, at movies, on television, etc.). Practice listening for speech patterns, tone, and voice. Copy some of the dialogues you hear into your journal.

— Look carefully at the dialogues in whatever you are reading. What works, what doesn't work? Learn from seeing how other writers handle dialogue.

— Make your dialogue sound natural. Be direct; order it in beats, as in scripts, letting the dialogue proceed beat by beat. Avoid lengthy dialogues.

— Be attentive to rhythm. Look at speech patterns, the length of words and sentences. Consider how to use hesitations and repetition.

— Read dialogue aloud until it sounds the way the speaker would say it. Make each voice distinctive. The reader should know who is speaking from the cadence, the choice of words, and the rhythm of each character's speech.

And don't overlook indirect dialogue. It often introduces, condenses, and complements direct dialogue. Pay also attention to what is not said. This is the subtext, the hidden dialogue that amplifies the spoken dialogue. Above all, practice. Write short dialogues and read them with a friend. Rehearse them as scripts. You are onstage.

WRITING A DIALOGUE

For this exercise, I suggest that you imagine a mini-story, in fiction or nonfiction, written almost entirely in dialogue. First find a character who wants something deeply. A child who wants his parents to stop fighting. An adolescent who wants to quit school to play the piano. An adult who wants to leave a relationship in order to live with someone else. An older adult who wants to see his or her children more often. Someone with a strong desire. Remember the Hemingway story: the man wanting the girl to stay with him. Remember the McBride story: the young boy wanting to understand why his mother is crying. If it is an imagined character, it will necessarily be fiction. If it is a remembered character, or yourself, you can choose whether to write it as fiction or nonfiction.

✎ Exercise: Write a short character sketch of your protagonist. Five minutes.

Once you have this character, find the second character to whom he is speaking. Let this secondary character oppose him, as in the excerpts from Hemingway and McBride. Ask yourself what his reasons are to stand in the way. A dialogue is a meaningful exchange between two characters. Who is this secondary character? You have to understand him.

✎ Exercise: Write a brief character sketch of your secondary character, playing the antagonist. Five minutes.

Now set the scene of the confrontation. In a few lines describe where the dialogue will take place—a few details to show the place. You may not use this when you write your dialogue, but it is important that you the writer know the setting. Then introduce the characters. Bring them onstage. Again, in a few lines give one or two familiar details from your character sketches.

✎ Exercise: Set the scene and introduce the characters. Five minutes.

Think about what your main character hopes to obtain in this one encounter. Will there be a step forward or a step backward? Whatever happens, your main character has to be moved at the end. The dialogue has to bring a revelation. Imagine the confrontation. Start to write the dialogue. Write slowly and let the dialogue reveal your two characters. Include hidden dialogue, gestures, pauses.

✎ Exercise: Start to write the dialogue. Ten minutes.

Stop and read what you have written. Remember the three purposes of dialogue: reveal the characters, advance the plot, contribute to the tone. Is each character's voice unique, revealing the speaker? Does the story move forward? Has the dialogue contributed to the tone, to creating the atmosphere of the encounter? And finally, has the main character changed, gained a new awareness? Now rewrite the dialogue, remembering that it's a mini-story with a beginning, a middle, an end.

✎ Exercise: Rewrite your dialogue, remembering it's a
mini-story. Ten minutes. When you are finished, again
take a moment to give it a title. Naming gives each piece
respect and counters the tendency to belittle your work.

At the beginning of this lesson, we defined dialogue as "an effective exchange of meaningful ideas." This is what your short dialogue has aimed to do. If your character has been able to come to grips with his or her desire—even in the slightest way—the dialogue has been meaningful.

Now for a last exercise that is both fun and very effective. Share your dialogue with another writer, either in a workshop setting or with a writing partner. Choose which character you will each play and read aloud. This is practice for writing scripts. As mentioned earlier, good dialogue proceeds by beats, one response after another. Try standing up when you read; you will hear the dialogue better. Encourage one another. Imagine yourselves onstage. Often, when I teach dialogue and include this exercise, I will ask if there are a few partners who wish to read. They come up and stand in front of their audience. The short scripts are amazing, and there is applause!

✎ Exercise: Share your dialogue with another writer; read it aloud. Ten minutes.

✎ This lesson contains three five-minute exercises and three longer, ten-minute ones. You may follow them one after another. Or if you wish to work more slowly: over the course of the month you may do the first three short ones (the two character sketches and setting the scene) during the first week, then the longer exercises (starting the dialogue, rewriting it, sharing it), one each week.

Tales: Folk, Fairy, and Contemporary

Folk tales—or fairy tales as they were later called—both enchant and enliven. When I find myself surrounded by mischievous grandchildren, if I offer to tell them a story and start with the words, "Once upon a time, there was . . ." they immediately settle down, sit on the floor, put their hands together, and listen, as if charmed. This new lesson brings together the earlier lessons of writing short stories, writing from dreams, writing dialogues, and weaves them together into writing tales.

Fairy tales and the very words "Once upon a time . . ." have acquired over the ages an ingrained fascination. They carry a power that surprises, that leads us to our center. They dip into our unconscious and bring forth archetypal elements from our early origins that touch our emotions and set our imaginations on fire. The listener knows that a story is coming. Will the prince find the princess? Will the children find their way home or will the witch pop them into the oven? Will the frog give back the golden ball?

Every people has its own sagas and miraculous stories that migrate from one village to another, becoming folk or fairy tales that can be handed on and easily remembered. We have inherited these stories from our parents and grandparents over the centuries, back to when our ancestors sat around the fire and shared their tales. They constitute an immense treasure chest that is ours to open.

DEFINITIONS

These treasures of folklore are more aptly called folk tales, as indeed they were until the seventeenth century when the term "fairy tale" took hold. In *Merriam-Webster's Collegiate Dictionary,* fairy tale is defined as a narrative of adventures, involving fantastic forces and beings (i.e., fairies, wizards, and goblins). In *In the Ever After: Fairy Tales and the Second Half of Life,* Allan B. Chinen defines a fairy tale as a folk tale, most often with a happy ending, featuring human beings in unusual situations struggling with basic human dilemmas. Folk tales are traditional stories of universal interest; hence, the same ones can be found around the world.

In depth psychology fairy tales are seen as expressions of a personal quest to achieve deeper awareness. They are stories that illustrate our impulse toward a greater level of consciousness. You listen to them as you listen to your dreams. You befriend them, amplify their themes, enter into them, and act out their characters. In "Little Red Riding Hood," you are the little girl carrying a basket to your grandmother, not listening to your mother, straying from the path, entering the woods. Each story is the reflection of a human reality that comes up over and over in our lives.

These realities are beyond centuries and cultures. They are time-less and place-less. This illuminates the key difference between folk tales and myths. Myths are bound by their cultures; they contain specific cultural additions. In the Greek myths, for example, Zeus, Apollo, and Athena are not only characters in stories the Greeks listened; they are gods and goddesses to whom the Greeks prayed. Consider Athena's immense statue that once reigned in the Parthenon in Athens.

Likewise, fables are different from fairy tales. Fables are traditionally short tales containing a moral in which the characters are animals. I say traditionally, for there are exceptions. Italo Calvino wrote fables with people as characters *(The Man Who Shouted Teresa)*, as do Eduardo Galeano *(The Book of Embraces)*, James Thurber *(Fables for Our Time)*, and George Orwell *(Animal Farm)*.

But as always, definitions are flexible. How should *The Lion, the Witch, and the Wardrobe* by C.S. Lewis, be classified? In his dedication, Lewis said it was a fairy tale.

My Dear Lucy,

I wrote this story for you, but when I began it I had not realized that girls grow quicker than books. As a result you are already too old for fairy tales, and by the time it is printed and bound you will be older still. But some day you will be old enough to start reading fairy tales again. You can then take it down from some upper shelf, dust it, and tell me what you think of it. I shall probably be too deaf to hear, and too old to understand a word you say, but I shall still be

your affectionate Godfather, C.S. Lewis

However, this same story is also seen today as an allegory because of the Christian drama that it contains, in which Aslan the Lion is a figure for Christ. It may also be seen as a fable because the animals speak, and because it contains a moral. So much for definitions.

HISTORY OF FAIRY TALES

Some scholars consider "Cupid and Psyche" by Apuleius, in the second century to be the first literary fairy tale. Continuing forward very briefly in history, there is the Hindu collection of tales, *Panchatantra,* in the fourth century, many of which are often seen as forerunners of the European fairy tales. The first version of Cinderella was written in Chinese in the ninth century. Then in the sixteenth century, *One Thousand and One Arabian Nights* was first recorded, with tales from Arabia, Persia, India, and Egypt.

Until the seventeenth century, fairy tales were appreciated among all ages, especially in the popular layers of society. Our elders remembered old myths and tales and told them in everyday language. These tales related local sagas, family incidents, and stories of their dreams. Then the nomenclature "fairy tales" took hold, perhaps in part due to the popularity of tales written by female writers in the French salons and named *Contes des Fées* (stories of fairies). Once named fairy tale, they were considered by some to be destined for a younger audience.

In 1697 there appeared Charles Perrault's collection, *Contes de ma Mère l'Oye, (Tales of Mother Goose)*, including "Cinderella," "Little Red Riding Hood," and "Bluebeard." Jacob and Wilhelm Grimm followed in 1819 with their very large collection, *Tales for Young and Old,* including "Hansel and Gretel," "Snow

White," and "Rumplestiltskin." Many of the same tales are in both collections. The Grimms' collection had such immense success that it led to a revision of Perrault's collection and to collections of national tales.

In the early nineteenth century, also in Europe, Hans Christian Andersen was writing and rendering tales of his own — "The Ugly Duckling," "The Little Match Girl," "The Emperor's New Clothes" among many others. Around the same time Washington Irving published the first American tales, with *Rip Van Winkle* (adapted from the German fairy tale *Karl Katz* by the Brothers Grimm) and *The Legend of Sleepy Hollow* (his own fictional folk tale) in 1820.

Enter the twentieth century. Walt Disney's first adaptation of a fairy tale was "Snow White and the Seven Dwarfs" in 1937. J.R.R. Tolkien published *The Hobbit* the same year, and a decade later, *Lord of the Rings*. Anthologies of stories and poems based on fairy tale motifs followed from Anne Sexton and Angela Carter. Then J.K. Rowling gave life to Harry Potter in 1997. Today hundreds of millions of copies of the Harry Potter books have been sold. The tale continues to nourish our imagination.

THE STRUCTURE OF FAIRY TALES

Fairy tales include the three basic parts of a story as discussed in Lesson Four:

— In the beginning, something happens to a character, creating a need or a desire.

— In the middle, as the character pursues his need, he meets an adversary; a struggle follows.

— In the end, the character is moved, with a resolution (transformation).

Here is a Grimm fairy tale, "The Three Feathers," the way I tell it to my grandchildren. Remember, there are many versions of each tale, depending upon who is the storyteller and who is the audience.

"The Three Feathers"

Once upon a time there was a king with three sons. Two of the sons were clever, but the youngest didn't talk much and was called Dummling. It was time for the king to choose which son would inherit the kingdom. So he told them to go out into the world and whoever brought him the most beautiful carpet would be king. To prevent any quarrels, he took them outside and blew three feathers, saying "Go as they fly."

One feather went east, one went west, and one fell to the ground straight ahead. One brother went to the right, one to the left, and Dummling sat down and sighed. All of a sudden he saw a trap door beside the feather. He lifted it, found steps, and went down into the earth. He came to another door and knocked. The door opened, and there sat a big fat toad surrounded by a circle of little toads. The fat toad asked him what he wanted. Dummling said he needed a beautiful carpet. Whereupon the toad opened a big box and handed him the most beautiful carpet on earth. Dummling thanked her and went back up the steps to the king.

The two older brothers had brought back simple shawls from shepherdesses. When the king saw Dummling's beautiful carpet, he said, "The kingdom goes to the youngest." But the two brothers made such a fuss that the king set another contest. This time they were to bring him the most beautiful ring. Again the king blew the three feathers. One went east, one went west, and the third one fell to the ground. One brother went to the right, one to the left, and Dummling hurried back to the toad and told her this time he needed a beautiful ring. The toad opened the big box and gave him the most beautiful ring on earth.

The two older brothers had brought back simple cart wheels. And when the king saw Dummling's gold ring, he said, "The kingdom goes to the youngest." But the two brothers made still a bigger fuss, and the king set still another contest. This time they were to bring him the most beautiful maiden. He blew the three feathers and they flew as before. Dummling rushed back to the toad and said he needed a beautiful maiden. She said that soon the maiden would appear and gave him a hollowed-out carrot with six harnessed mice. She told him to put one of the little toads into the carrot. No sooner had he done so than the little toad turned into the most beautiful maiden on earth, the carrot into a coach, and the six mice into six horses. Dummling thanked the toad, kissed the maiden and drove away to the king.

The two older brothers had brought back simple peasant women. When the king saw Dummling's beautiful maiden, he said, "The kingdom goes to the youngest." But the two older brothers deafened the king's ears, asking that the one whose maiden could jump through the ring hanging in the middle of the room be the next king. They thought that their peasant women with strong legs would succeed and the beautiful maiden would fall to her death. The old king agreed. The peasant women jumped but they were so heavy they fell and broke their arms and legs. Dummling's maiden sprang as lightly as a deer through the ring.

After that, Dummling got the crown and ruled in wisdom for many years.

The three-part structure is evident. The first part opens with the king growing old and needing to choose one son to succeed him. The second part relates how the youngest son wins each of the three tests, finding the woven cloth, the ring, and the most beautiful maiden. Then there is the fourth test, asking his wife to jump through the hoop. The third part, written in one sentence, resolves the situation with the youngest son proclaimed king and ruling wisely for many years.

Also evident are many typical characteristics of the fairy tale. First there is a king and three sons, and the time when the king must name his successor. Then there are the three tests: the carpet, the ring, and the lady. Here is the classical motif of three in the fairy tale. But there is also a fourth test—jumping through the hoop. Marie-Louise von Franz writes in *The Interpretation of Fairy Tales* that a fourth test is also a typical rhythm in fairy tales. There are three similar testings and then a final action. The first three lead up to the fourth, which is the climax and ushers in the resolution. There are also helpers along the way: the big fat toad and her little toads. There is magic. There are the trap door and the big box, the fine carpet, the beautiful ring. The carrot becomes a coach, the six mice become six horses, and the little toad becomes the beautiful woman. And there is the happy ending. Dummling gets the crown and rules with wisdom for many years.

For a moment, hold on to the tale, the way you hold on to a dream, not to interpret it, but rather to experience the story, to imagine it on the stage, and to enter into it. Jung called this "active imagination." "You must enter into the process with your personal reactions, just as if you were one of the fantasy figures, as if the drama being enacted before your eyes were real." (*Mysterium Coniunctionis,* Paragraph 706)

Sit back and actively imagine the fairy tale. Are you the old king, looking for a successor? The father or the mother, testing your children? Or are you one of the children, the oldest defending your birthright? Or the youngest, finding the trap door in the ground and descending down into the earth? Or are you the big fat toad, or the little toad, the helper, always helping? Imagine yourself as one of the characters in the story. Relive the tale.

And now write down what it felt like in a short journal entry. Some words like, "Upon reading 'The Three Feathers,' I imagined myself to be Dummling. I saw the trapdoor and opened it." What did it feel like to go into the dark? It is important to write down where a fairy tale takes you in your imagination and feelings. People have been listening to this tale for centuries. There is a field of energy around it. As you tap into it, your senses are stimulated. You become richer, your writing becomes richer. Without writing it down, you may forget it.

✎ Exercise: Write a short journal entry on reading "The Three Feathers." Five minutes.

THE SUBJECT MATTER OF FAIRY TALES
The subject matter of fairy tales is as varied as our lives. However, if we look at the ages of the characters, we will see three different age cycles, each one ending with a different type of transformation. In her workshop on the fairy tale, writer and instructor Susan Baugh describes these groupings:

— Youth tales: The young character leaves home and family, seeks true love or treasure, fights evil, and

      develops a strong will. The transformation focuses
      on *adaptation*.
— Midlife tales: The character gives up youthful
      thinking, confronts tragedy, and develops a sense of
      self. The transformation focuses on *renewal*.
— Elder tales: The character transcends worldly view-
      points, reclaims youthful innocence, confronts death,
      and develops wisdom. The transformation focuses on
      illumination and *mediation* (between generations).

"The Three Feathers" is a youth tale, with the third son, Dummling, seeking treasure and learning to adapt to the world around him.

Now the second tale will be an elder tale: "The Six Statues," included in Alan B. Chinen's collection *In the Ever After: Fairy Tales and the Second Half of Life*. Instead of focusing on growing up, these tales focus on growing old, and more importantly on growing psychologically and spiritually.

"THE SIX STATUES"

Once upon a time, there lived a kind old man and woman who were very poor. One New Year's Eve, they found they had no money to buy rice cakes for the holiday. Then they remembered seven straw hats the old man had made some time before. "I shall go to the village to sell them," the old man said. So his wife put one of the hats on his head, and the other six on his shoulders, and off he went in the snow.

All that day the old man tried peddling his hats, but no one bought any. So late in the afternoon, he trudged up to the snowy trail back to his house, wrapped in misery. On his way, he noticed six statues of gods, standing in the snow. They were the guardian deities of children and looked so cold and lonely that the old man paused. "I cannot leave you to shiver here!" he exclaimed, and so he gave each statue a straw hat, tying them carefully on the gods' heads. Then the old man returned home.

The old woman sighed when her husband told her he had no rice cakes. But she smiled when he described giving his hats to the six statues. "Imagine how happy they must be!" she exclaimed. Later that night, after a meager New Year's Eve dinner, the old man and his wife went to bed.

At midnight, they were awakened by strange noises outside their house. "Who could that be?" the old man exclaimed. They listened and made out the sound of people singing.

At that moment, the door flew open, and a bag landed in the middle of their hut. It fell open, revealing the prettiest rice cakes the old man and his wife had ever seen, smelling sweet and fresh. And when they looked through their door, they saw six statues, each with a straw hat, bowing a New Year's greeting to them!

Before looking at the different parts of the tale, try to put yourself into the story; relive it in your imagination. Watch the old man and woman decide together that he should sell the seven straw hats. Then watch the old man after leaving the market, as he carefully ties a hat on each of the stone gods' heads. Be the old man who stops to talk to statues, or the old woman who does not get angry when her husband comes home empty-handed. Or be the statue who comes to life.

Then write it down. What happened in imagining "The Six Statues"? How did it feel to talk to stone statues, to rediscover the mystery that surrounds us, the almost mystical experience of living the present moment?

✎ Exercise: Write a short journal entry about reading
  "The Six Statues." Five minutes.

As we learned earlier, in the elder tale, the focus is on illumina-
tion, on enlightenment. The old man and the old woman
encounter magic and rediscover a childlike awe in the presence
of the six statues. The rest of their lives will be illuminated by
it. And the six statues, as guardian deities of children, will continue to mediate between the generations.

WRITING CONTEMPORARY TALES

In writing contemporary tales, you look for the core story of the
fairy tale and ask yourself how someone today would react to
this situation. What might change in the tale? What variations
would be forthcoming? And what universal truths would
remain the same? Here is an example of a modern tale by writer
Lynne Barrett, published in *River City Magazine,* 2005. It is a
modern take on "Little Red Riding Hood"—and a bold one,
written in second person.

"LITTLE RED RETURNS"

These days you are a strawberry blonde. Back in town after
a long rest at a woodland spa, peace, yoga, massages, excellent
sleep in a rustic cottage, you feel ready. Tonight you're with
a backwoodsman you picked up out there, young, stalwart,
unblemished. You take him clubbing, enjoying his astonishment as you go from one dizzy crowd to the next.

    Wouldn't you know it, you run into Vülf, entering Fungi
as you leave.

    "Where are you going, my dear?" His deep voice catches

you, the same growl that, intoning on records, drew all the little girls, including you, back when.

"Oh, you know," you tell him, "we have to take it all in. We're headed to Anni's party at Rose Red, later on."

"Ah, Anni's party. I'll be there," he says, "my dear." His rasp raises the hair on your neck.

You want the old Vülf to swallow you and you know it. You've been in that darkness before. When you were with him his world surrounded you. You traveled with his pack and wore clothes he designed, the chic of the hood. You shared his nightly wandering, lived on his diet of steak and Veuve Clicquot and coca, went back to his lair and, while his music pounded around you, shook to his snarls. You cried, didn't you, when he threw you away? You've dreamed of him, haven't you: tall, charcoal and silver.

At Anni's party, he's not there. Anni herself has made more than one comeback and the white streak in her black hair seems now to be the only natural thing about her. The young models call her Granny, but still she reigns. The club is a hall of flattering pink mirrors. At one end, the bar glows, its long curve of rose-etched glass lit from within. You dance with your woodsman, turning and turning till you catch a glimpse of Vülf.

He beckons and you go to his red velvet corner. He offers you your choice, but you take the same mineral water that he's having.

He pours it and grins. His smile is dark.

"Why, Vülf, what happened to that big tooth you had?"

"Ah, the diamond fang. You remember that, sweetheart? I cashed it in. You heard I had a patch of trouble, no doubt."

"I heard something about those arms you had."

"The his and hers Uzis under the back seat? They were quite legal, I had the papers, but certain parties were looking for an excuse to take me down. Fortunately, a whisper reached me."

"I know what sharp ears you had."

"They thought they'd snare me on a weapons count. They impounded everything they could get their hands on, but in the end found nothing to charge me with, my dear. I had to sell a few little items," that dark grin again, "but I'm safe."

"Are you sure? Once they go after you-"

"Why? What have you heard?" His long face looks at you slyly, warily.

"Not a thing. So you're back in business?"

"Oh yes, I'm cooking up a sweet production deal. My strength, you know, has always been sensing what new wildness kids have in them."

"Everyone knows what an eye you have for talent."

"That's right. Indeed, I'm on the prowl tonight to see what I can find. So happy to come upon *you,* my dear. I think perhaps it's you I overlooked before."

But you know better. You have no talent. And if he's considering you, looking at you fondly—fondly!—patting your hand, well, he's no good to you any more.

You smile and squeeze his hairy wrist and go find your woodsman on the dance floor, surrounded by famished beauties. You carry him off, out into the early morning starlight. You run your hand along his strong young arm. While you still can, you howl.

"In telling and retelling stories," writes Barrett, "we work out permutations, drawing on what they've meant to us and recasting what strikes us as less true to some truth of our own."

She has recast the woodsman and the grandmother (Anni), and there is a second permutation: no longer is Vülf dangerous, but it is Little Red who needs taming.

Our exercise will now be to write a contemporary tale imagined or drawn from our own life or someone else's. Go within and find a character and an experience—real or imagined—that ask to be written as a tale. If the character is young, it will be a youth tale, with the character perhaps leaving home, encountering an adversary, learning to adapt to the world around him. If the character is older, it will be a midlife tale, with the character giving up youthful thinking and developing a sense of self. If the character is still older, it will be an elder tale, with the character growing in wisdom, listening to stone statues.

Because all of us have an instinct for storytelling, when we start with "Once upon a time . . ." we will intuitively find our way through the story to the resolution. Remember the three parts of the story.

— A beginning: Something happens—a character creates a desire or need.
— A middle: The protagonist struggles against an adversary, up to and including the climax.
— An end, the story's fulfillment: Out of the climax comes a new awareness.

As you start this exercise, think about your character in the third person, as "he" or "she" If you are writing from your own experience, this will give you some distance, letting you see it as story. Fairy tales are almost always written in the third person.

If you are in a workshop setting, share your tale briefly with the person next to you. When you talk to someone, you naturally shape the story to make it more interesting. And as I have said in earlier chapters, if the listener loses interest, then find another character. If you are not in a workshop setting, again see if you can find a friend to listen to your story. This sharing creates energy that stimulates the storyteller and guides him through the telling. When done well, it keeps the story within bounds.

WRITING YOUR TALE

Now start writing your tale. Begin with "Once upon a time . . ." or with another traditional beginning, time-less and place-less. Remember, it can be short. Do not rush. I propose suggested times that fit the chapter structure, but these times can be extended. Your writing will benefit.

✎ Exercise: Begin your fairy tale with the words, "Once upon a time . . .." Ten minutes.

Stop after ten minutes. You should be into the middle part of the story. What is the struggle? Stretch a bit, breathe deeply. How does your character confront the adversary? Return to your writing. Catch up or slow down and continue writing through the struggle to the climax.

✎ Exercise: Continue writing through the middle part of your tale. Ten minutes.

Stop after another ten minutes. You should be at the end of your tale. Have you discovered the resolution? Not just the ending, but the new awareness?

✎ Exercise: Continue writing through the resolution. Five
  minutes.

Reread your story and see if there is some element that can be
repeated three times. Are there three testings, three different
helpers? Circle an element that can be repeated three times.

✎ Exercise: Work in one repetition of three. Five minutes.

Before ending this exercise, take a moment to look at your first
sentence. Remember the first sentences of our three tales:
  "There was once a king who had three sons . . ."
  "Once upon a time, there lived a kind old man and woman
who were very poor."
  "These days you are a strawberry blond . . ."
  Say them aloud, hear their rhythms, listen to the cadence of
the syllables (the meter, the repeated stressed and unstressed
syllables). Now read your first sentence. Read it aloud. Does it
have rhythm? Does it have a regular beat?

✎ Exercise: Work on your first sentence. Five minutes.

Finally, find the title for it. Take your time. Of course the title
may change. But for now, what is the title of your fairy tale?

✎ Exercise: Write the title, and underneath write your name.
  Skip a line and write the revised first sentence. This is the
  beginning of your tale. Five minutes.

If you are in a group of writers, this would be the right time and
place to go around the group, with each writer giving the title—

and the first sentence if there is time—of his or her tale. When you share the titles, you share your energy and give life to your tales.

Now put your tale aside and when you have time, reread it and continue to rewrite it. It is your tale, to be remembered and refined and repeated.

✎ In this lesson, there are two short exercises of five minutes each: writing a journal entry about reading a fairy tale. Then there is a long guided exercise in parts that total forty minutes as you write your own tale. You can follow the exercises as suggested in a single lesson. Or you could do the first two exercises the first week, then the rest of the writing could be done over three weeks: the first part of the tale; the second part of the tale, then the remaining shorter exercises (working in a repetition of three, polishing the first sentence, giving a title) together.

Poetic Prose and the Prose Poem

L esson Two briefly introduced the elements of poetry in essay writing. Here you will work with them at length, writing poetic prose in many different forms, focusing especially on the prose poem.

Poetic prose sounds like a paradox, poetry being defined as what is not prose and prose being defined as what is not poetry. Yet the two are much closer than you might think at first. Charles Baudelaire, introducing his *Petites Poèmes en Prose* in 1855, wrote, "Which of us, in his ambitious moments, has not dreamed of the miracle of a poetic prose . . . supple and rugged enough to adapt itself to the lyrical impulses of the soul." We dream of poetic prose and we write it. As long as our words come from within, study and practice will bring a heightened capacity to make them resonate. The skills of prose writers are very much the same as the skills of poets. Susan Vreeland, author of *The Girl in Hyacinth Blue,* writes that bits of poetry and scenes crafted with paint and words come together in her work. "With this polishing comes the refinement of voice, the unexpected uncovering of inter-relatedness."

TWO EXAMPLES BY WAY OF INTRODUCTION

Here are two examples of poetic prose—one nonfiction, the other fiction—by way of introduction. The nonfiction example is from an essay by Patricia Hampl about memory and imagination, how imagination is necessary not only to shape the memory but to find its meaning. In polishing your writing—in using elements of poetry—you uncover its essence. The second example is from the novel *Snow* by Orhan Pamuk. The primary metaphor, snow, resonates in the reader's heart. Both examples will be used throughout this lesson as you study the elements of poetry.

First is the opening of the essay, "Memory and Imagination," in Patricia Hampl's collection entitled *I Could Tell You Stories.*

From "Memory and Imagination"

When I was seven, my father, who played the violin on Sundays with a nicely tortured flair which we considered artistic, led me by the hand down a long, unlit corridor in St. Luke's School basement, a sort of tunnel that ended in a room full of pianos. There, many little girls and a single sad boy were playing truly tortured scales and arpeggios in a mash of troubled sound. My father gave me over to Sister Olive Marie, who did look remarkably like an olive.

Her oily face gleamed as if it had just been rolled out of a can and laid on the white plate of her broad, spotless wimple . . .

I was shown middle C, which Sister seemed to think terribly important. I stared at middle C, and then glanced away for a second. When my eye returned, middle C was gone, its slim finger lost in the complicated grasp of the keyboard. Sister Olive struck it again with laughable ease. She emphasized the importance of middle C, its central position, a sort of North Star of sound. I remember thinking, middle C is the belly button of the piano, an insight whose originality and accuracy stunned me with pride. For the first time in my life I was astonished by metaphor. I hesitated to tell the kindly Olive for some reason; apparently I understood a true metaphor is a risky business, revealing of the self. In fact, I have never, until this moment of writing it down, told my first metaphor to anyone.

Sunlight flooded the room; the pianos, all black, gleamed. Sister Olive, dressed in the colors of the keyboard, gleamed; middle C shimmered with meaning and I resolved never—never—to forget its location: It was the center of the world.

We will look at this passage in detail later, but for now let's just enjoy it: the descriptive details, the rhythm of the sentences, the images, and the narrator's own discovery of metaphor as a young child.

The second example is from the first page of *Snow* by Orhan Pamuk, the story of the return of the poet Ka to Turkey after a long political exile in Germany. He is traveling from Istanbul to Kars, on the other side of the country.

FROM "THE SILENCE OF SNOW"

The silence of snow, thought the man sitting just behind the bus-driver. If this were the beginning of a poem, he would have called what he felt inside him "the silence of snow."

He'd boarded the bus from Erzurum to Kars with only seconds to spare. . .

As soon as the bus set off, our traveler glued his eyes to the window next to him. Perhaps hoping to see something new, he peered into the wretched little shops, the bakeries and broken-down coffee-houses that lined the streets of Erzurum's outlying suburbs, and as he did, it began to snow. It was heavier and thicker than the snow he'd seen between Istanbul and Erzurum. If he hadn't been so tired, if he'd paid more attention to the snowflakes swirling out of the sky like feathers, he might have realized that he was traveling straight into a blizzard; he might have seen from the start that he had set out on a journey that would change his life for ever; he might have turned back. But the thought didn't even cross his mind. As evening fell, he lost himself in the light still lingering in the sky above. In the snowflakes whirling ever more wildly in the wind he saw nothing of the impending blizzard, but rather a promise, a sign pointing back to the happiness and purity he had once known as a child.

Again, for now, simply take pleasure in the writing, the scene, feeling the snowflakes as they grow heavier and thicker, a promise of purity, yet with a shadow of impending gloom, far from the happiness of his childhood.

As you return to these passages during the pages ahead, immerse yourself in the poetic writing. Let yourself appreciate the sounds, the melody, the figurative language, the similes, the metaphors.

This lesson asks you to first look at two elements of poetic prose, rhythm and imagery, keeping in mind that there is another important element of poetry: compression. In writing poetic prose, you pay attention to rhythm and imagery, and with practice you learn to compress: to get rid of all extra words, of all extra sentences. It is like distilling. You eliminate all that distracts from your purpose. You compress. You will work more with compression in the second part of the lesson, dealing with the prose poem.

THE ELEMENT OF RHYTHM

Rhythm in writing means to make resonant. *Merriam-Webster's Collegiate Dictionary* defines rhythm as the flow of sound and silence. Just as in music where the rests (the pauses) are essential, so it is in writing. It cannot all be sound. There has to be silence. E.M. Forster in *Aspects of the Novel* defines rhythm as "repetition plus variation." A writer attentive to sound hears the rhythmic ebb and flow in his mind even before he writes the words. Likewise, the reader, without moving his lips, hears the same rhythmic ebb and flow when he reads the words.

As a writer of prose, how do you create a rhythmic flow in your writing? Here are three ways: meter, word sounds, and "extra voltage."

Meter

Meter is basic to the rhythm of the writing and asks the writer to pay attention to the melody of each sentence. Writing is like Lord Krishna's flute, in that it expresses the invisible music of the heart. John Gardner, in *The Art of Fiction,* writes about poetic rhythm and gives a lesson in verse scansion (reading with an eye to meter, scanning) for prose writers. Insisting that rhythm and variation are as basic to prose as to poetry, Gardner shows how the fairly regular occurrence of stressed and unstressed syllables makes for stronger writing. It is his belief that good prose differs in only one way from good contemporary verse (meaning free verse—unrhymed and metrically irregular), and that is line breaks. Verse slows the reader by means of line breaks; prose does not.

Let's look again at the two passages we read earlier.

Listen to the opening words from Hampl's excerpt: "When I was seven, my father who played the violin on Sundays with a nicely tortured flair which we considered artistic, led me by the hand . . ." Now copy the first sentence, putting it in syllables and place a mark (') after each syllable that is stressed. Here is how I read it: When I' was sevn' my fa' ther who played' the vi' o lin' on Sun' days with' a nice' ly tor' tured flair' led' me by' the hand'

As you read this aloud, you hear the regular beat of short / long, short / long, short / long. This beat is called iambic. Its regularity is comforting. You the reader want to hold on to some of the words, "my fa' ther led' me by' the hand'," with four strong iambic beats. This is a rhythm that Robert Frost used often: "Whose woods these are I think I know." Looking at the Hampl quote, you can also see that the iambic rhythm is twice broken. There are two unstressed syllables together in the first line (ther who played'), and two stressed syllables in the second line (flair' led'). This too is important. If it had all been iambic, the rhythm would have been monotonous.

Now listen to the first four words in the passage from Pamuk. "The silence of snow." Five beats, short-long-long-short-long:

the si' lence' of snow'. In scanning these words, the reader wants to clap five times. And the four words are used in the title of the chapter, to begin the first sentence and end the second sentence. The rhythm is set in the reader's mind. Three times the same four words are repeated. The reader enters the silence along with Ka. The silence of snow.

As a writer, you learn to pay attention to meter. It becomes part of your voice. Joan Didion writes in her memoir *A Year of Magical Thinking* that even as a young writer, she discovered that meaning resided in the rhythm of her words and sentences. Listen to your own writing. Stand up and read the first page of an essay or short story. Reading aloud is good practice, and it is good to stand up when you do. You will breathe more deeply. You will hear your own voice—where it is confident and where it is less so.

Write just one or two lines about a snowstorm. And write it in iambic (unstressed/stressed) meter. Perhaps with four stressed syllables (in poetic language these are called feet) in your line: this meter is called tetrameter. Or with five stressed syllables, called pentameter. Here is an example of iambic pentameter, "The snow storm swirled around me in the street." There are five stressed syllables: short / long, short / long, short / long, short / long, short / long. Here it is written in syllables, with the stressed syllables marked: The snow' storm swirled' a round' me in' the street'.

Now it's your turn. Try your hand at one or two lines of metered prose.

✎ Exercise: write one sentence in iambic pentameter. Five minutes.

Word Sounds

Another way to put rhythm into prose is through onomatopoeia—word sounds, the musical accompaniment to words. You see the word and you hear it: a picture with sound, for example, the whistling wind (you hear the wind) or the fizzling fire (you hear the fire.) Even single words can be word sounds. Words like "crunch" (you again hear the sound, almost closing your teeth), "smear" (you hear it and you feel it), "hollow" (the sound itself is hollow). You can train yourself to look for word sounds when you read. The more you grow aware of them, the more you will find them in your own writing. Your writing intensifies and becomes stronger.

Let's look at examples of word sounds in the two excerpts.

In Hampl's essay about her first piano lesson, there is a "tortured flair;" the word "tortured" sounds tortured. The reader cannot read it, say it, or see it without feeling tortured. Then "a mash of troubled sound": the reader hears the piano mash coming from the tortured scales and arpeggios. The word is usually associated with potatoes, but here it is associated with pianos. There follows the image of the olive rolling out of the can. The word "roll" sounds like something rolling and the "l" lingers in the mouth. Still further along, we are "astonished by metaphor." The reader not only sees the word "astonished," but hears the astonishment of a seven-year-old girl.

Now on the opening page of Pamuk's novel, there is "the silence of snow." The reader hears the silence. The word 'silence' sounds like what it describes. The two evenly stressed syllables, si_- lence_, contribute to this, as does the "s" sound at the beginning and the end. The reader reads the word and is silenced. Then "snowflakes swirling": the word "swirl" cannot be said without emitting air—a word sound. And then "blizzard" not "storm". Another word sound. The reader hears the two z's, the blizzard.

Again it is your turn. Think about word sounds in your writing. Continue with the snowflakes, imagine a snow storm. Or a music lesson. Find words that sound like what you are describing. Learn to come up with your own word sounds.

✎ Exercise: Write a few word sounds. Five minutes.

EXTRA VOLTAGE

A third way to put rhythm into your prose is through adding extra voltage. Seamus Heaney used these words to describe the poetic technique of heightening the sound of language. We can give extra voltage through alliteration—the repetition of consonants, of the same consonantal sound—and assonance—the repetition of vowels, of the same vowel sound. We can also give extra voltage by repetition of words. Here are some examples in the two excerpts:

Alliteration and Assonance

In Hampl's piece, listen to the "d"s in "led me by the hand down a long, unlit corridor." The repetition of this sound lets the reader follow the little girl, almost her footsteps, down the corridor. Then "the mash of troubled sound": the repetition of the different "o" sounds makes the mash still more troubled. There are also the "a"s and the "o"s in "astonished by metaphor," where there are only two of each, yet they play off one another.

In Pamuk's piece, listen again to the "s"s, "the silence of the snow." Then more "s"s in "snowflakes swirling out of the sky," and "w"s, with "snowflakes whirling ever more wildly in the wind." And listen to the "l"s in "he lost himself in the light still lingering . . ." The reader lingers, wanting to reread the sentence.

The repetition of these consonants and vowels gives more voltage to the prose. It is not accidental. The writing is crafted and polished.

Repetition

In the Hampl example, "middle C" is repeated five times in five sentences. The reader is centered on middle C. Then the word metaphor is repeated three times in the next three sentences. The repetition is purposeful. Next, the pianos gleamed. Sister Olive gleamed. And we remember a gleam from earlier and we look back: "Her oily face gleamed." The word "gleamed" is used three times.

In the Pamuk example, "The silence of snow" is repeated three times—in the title and the first two sentences. It sets the mood and foreshadows the theme. Then in the middle of the long paragraph, there is the triple repetition, "he might have . . . he might have . . . he might have." The reader is aware not only of the impending blizzard but of impending adversity.

Now write a few short lines, again describing a snowstorm or a music lesson, paying attention to the element of rhythm—meter, word sounds, and now alliteration and assonance. Look for repetition and variation.

✎ Exercise: Write a short paragraph describing a snowstorm or music lesson, paying attention to rhythm and
repetition. Ten minutes.

THE ELEMENT OF IMAGERY

Imagery in writing means to make visual. *Merriam-Webster's
Collegiate Dictionary* defines imagery as the art of making
mental pictures. Imagery stimulates the reader to look at
the subject matter in a new way. This leap in perspective is
at the center of imagery. In characterization, an image says
more than a long description. In the same way, imagery in a
setting contributes to the tone and mood, often foreshadowing what follows.

As you start to pay more attention to images in what you
read, look for ones that startle you, allowing you to see, taste, or
feel what the writer is describing. Note these images in your
journals and learn from them for your own writing. First there
are similes—figures of speech comparing two unlike things or
qualities usually introduced by "like" or "as." Then there are
metaphors—figures of speech comparing two unlike things or
qualities but without "like" or "as." And the deeper the
metaphor goes, the more symbolic it becomes. A metaphor that
dips into the unconscious to pull up deeper meaning becomes a
symbol. You have circled images in your writing from the earlier
chapters. Here you will move from image to simile to metaphor
to symbol.

Here is a simple example of the progression.

— Image: We start with a simple image, for example
"bright forsythia."
— Simile: To make the image more visual we use a simile:

"The blossoms shone as bright as gold." We see the blossoms.

— Metaphor: Next, we move to metaphor, staying with the image until we see it without "like" or "as." For example, "The golden blossoms set the bush aglow." We do not need to write that the blossoms made the bush look like (simile) it was glowing.

— Symbol: And then we move to symbol, linking the invisible and the visible. "The forsythia showed off its gold." There is a feeling of extravagance, so much gold that it was showed off. The metaphor of gold has taken on symbolic meaning.

Now let's look at similes and metaphors in the two excerpts.

Hampl's simile, "Sister Olive Marie, who looked remarkably like an olive," surprises us. Hampl continues, "Her oily face gleamed as if it had just been rolled out of a can and laid on the white plate of her broad spotless wimple." An olive on a white plate. Gleaming. The unusual simile hints at honesty, wholesomeness. Next, the middle C, "its slim finger was gone" (not the slim finger-like piano key, just its slim finger, is enough). It becomes the belly button of the piano. Hampl remembers that the metaphor astonished her. And she remembers that she hesitated to tell Sister Olive. Metaphors are risky. Symbolically, middle C is the center of her young world. A risky world.

With Pamuk's "Snow flakes swirling out of the sky like feathers," the reader sees the snow flakes, the feathers. There is a leap in perspective. Snowflakes to feathers. This leap is reinforced with the later image, "snowflakes whirling even more wildly in the wind . . ." Yet Ka does not see the impending blizzard. Rather, he sees the promise of the snowflakes, a sign pointing back to the happiness and purity of his childhood. In the contradictory imagery, the tone is set. The reader sees not only the impending blizzard, but the impending tragic thrust of the novel.

These two prose writers have followed their images into the unconscious, letting them bridge the visible world to the invisible world. By moving from image to simile to metaphor to symbol, the writers bring a new awareness of the image to the reader. The middle C of the keyboard, the swirling snowflakes—each image takes on deeper meaning. The reader is enriched and holds on to these images: each is pregnant with new life.

It is your turn to try. Just as when you wrote a short paragraph paying attention to rhythm, now write a short paragraph paying attention to images. You may wish to go back and reread the paragraph you wrote—about a music lesson or about snowflakes—in order to continue with it, but this time include similes and metaphors. But don't just add a simile; rework the passage, weave the visual images into the passage.

Or you may start another piece of writing. Take for example the blizzard; imagine yourself a young child in the middle of a snowstorm. What do the snowflakes feel like on your face? On the child's face? Write in the first person or distance yourself from the scene and write in the third person.

Remember that each time I suggest an exercise, I am asking you to write from within. Close your eyes. Go back to your childhood and remember a snowstorm. What images come to you? If another image calls to you instead, write about that. Look for similes and metaphors. Let the images lead you to something from within.

✎ Exercise: Write a paragraph, paying attention to similes
   and metaphors. Ten minutes.

You have written two short examples of poetic prose, one paying
attention to meter, the second paying attention to imagery. Now
you will look at compression, the third element of poetry,
focusing on the prose poem.

INTRODUCTION TO THE PROSE POEM

We will now focus on one particular form of poetic prose, the
prose poem. *Merriam-Webster's Collegiate Dictionary* defines
the prose poem as "a composition in prose that has some qualities of poetry, as rhythm, imagery, compactness of expression."
Because it is in prose, it does not have line breaks. Compactness
or compression, here is the essence of poetry. If you think of a
haiku—seventeen syllables—you can appreciate the importance
of compression. Compression is a process of distilling, a working
down to the essence.

To this definition I would add that a prose poem contains
paradox—a revelation of something with seemingly contradictory qualities. The medium of the prose poem is so flexible that
the writer can use it in many different genres, including fable,
travelogue, dreamscape, narrative fragment, reminiscence, and
burlesque. And almost always the prose poem resonates with a
desire for transcendence. It is this thrust to transcend that sus-
tains the prose poem and determines its form. All the details of
the poem are arranged so as to lead the reader to a sudden recognition of the "whatness" of something.

Here is a prose poem by Louis Jenkins, "A Quiet Place," from his
collection *Nice Fish*. In the preface Jenkins writes that it was the

freedom of the prose poem that first attracted him, allowing him to combine conscious narrative with images from the unconscious.

"A Quiet Place"

I have come to understand my love for you. I came to you like a man, world-weary, looking for a quiet place. The gas station and grocery store, the church, the abandoned school, a few old houses, the river with its cool shady spots . . . good fishing. How I've longed for a place like this! As soon as I got here I knew I'd found it. Tomorrow the set production and camera crews arrive. We can begin filming on Monday: the story of a man looking for a quiet place.

There is rhythm, imagery, compression, and paradox. From writing about the narrator's love, seen as a quiet place, Jenkins jumps to the grocery store, the church, "the river with its cool shady spots . . . good fishing" (the ellipsis is the poet's). There is conscious narrative followed by prosaic concrete images, then back to the conscious narrative: the narrator has longed for this place. Until the final leap—the set production, the camera crews, and the filming of the story of a man looking for a quiet place. The reader comes to a moment of understanding: the narrator knows his good fortune. So does the reader. Love ideally is a quiet place. Film it while it is there.

Prose poems are highly appreciated for their brevity, their poetry, and their paradox. They find their place in collections of poetry and in the traditional excellent literary reviews. Following on the heels of *The Prose Poem: An International Journal* is *Sentence: A Journal of Prose Poetics*. And now there are several online literary magazines for prose poetry: *Double Room, Cue,* and *Six Little Things*. Prose poems also find their place in works of literary nonfiction: Kathleen Norris's *Dakota,* Terry Tempest Williams' *Leap.* And Alice Walker's last page in her essay "My Mother's Blue Bowl" in *Anything We Love Can Be Saved* is a beautiful prose poem to her mother, "seemingly full forever," like the blue bowl that Walker found in the pantry.

The form of the prose poem is determined by its inner movement. There are prose poems that are one paragraph long, like little pockets containing a surprise. There are prose poems that are two pages long, rarely longer. Sometimes the page is one solid block of prose; other times the page is filled with short segments of prose. Naomi Shihab Nye sees them as "satisfying little house-shapes with windows and doors." Some prose poems are monologues, others are dialogues. Some are descriptive, others are all action. I have chosen two different types to work with: the narrative prose poem and the object prose poem.

THE NARRATIVE PROSE POEM

Narrative prose poems are often very close to flash fiction and the short-shorts you looked at in Lesson Four. These short paragraph-style pieces of writing are very visual, like short films. They establish a story line, then make an unexpected leap. They close with a logical conclusion, grounding the poem back in reality. The sequence travels from the rational to the irrational and back to the rational. This differentiates the prose poem from surrealism, where the poem would stay in the irrational. In a prose poem the reader is led back, albeit with a surprise. It differs from the short-short in its poetic quality. With the prose poem, you hear the poet speaking; the voice is more lyrical. With the short-short, you hear the storyteller speaking and the voice is more narrative.

Here is an example of a short narrative prose poem by Greg Boyd, from his collection *Carnival Aptitude*.

"Lovers"

Taking showers alone every day—that's not what life's all about—so a man carved himself a lover out of soap. Imagine his joy, his ecstasy at being wrapped in her slippery soft embrace. As for the rest, it's what one would expect: a steady melting away until, hand in hand, they disappeared together down the drain.

The story line is evident, a man takes his shower alone every day. He longs for company and fashions himself a lover out of a bar of soap. Then the unexpected leap—no longer does he feel alone; instead, he feels the warm embrace of the soap and is ecstatic. Then back we come to reality, as the soap melts and the dream, of the man and his lover, disappears down the drain. In Boyd's hands, the prose poem becomes a short lyrical film.

Look at how Boyd pays attention to the different elements of the prose poem:

— Rhythm: The poem opens swiftly—taking showers every day—as the reader quickly follows along. Then the rhythm slows up when the man carves a lover out of soap and is wrapped in her slippery soft embrace. The words are chosen to hold the reader back, to let him feel the embrace.

— Imagery: The image of the lovers is held in the reader's mind, until they melt away and disappear hand in hand tethered to the earth.

— Compression: Boyd has compressed his prose poem into fifty-one words.
— Paradox: From a man alone in the shower to the melting away of his dreams. It does not need to be spelled out.

Now it is your turn to write a prose poem with a strong narrative. Close your eyes and go within. What story comes to you? Instead of a man taking a shower, write perhaps about a man or woman falling asleep. Once you have the story, start to tell it in two or three sentences. Now let your imagination play. Close your eyes again. What might have happened? Let yourself be surprised. When the woman fell asleep, did white horses race through the bedroom? And then what? Return to the story, going back to where you were.

✎ Exercise: Start to write a narrative prose poem. Ten minutes. Remember to give your prose poem a title. And when you have time, go back and continue to work on it, to polish the rhythm and imagery. And compress.

THE OBJECT PROSE POEM

The object prose poem is best explained and illustrated by the contemporary poet Robert Bly. Here Bly takes an object and holds on to it—"holds on to its fur"—until it opens the door to the unconscious. In an interview with Peter Johnson, editor of *The Prose Poem: An International Journal* (Volume 7), Bly speaks of making leaps from the conscious to the unconscious, from the visible to the invisible. "My leaps have to do with a confidence that psychology gives me that one can see the invisible."

The pattern of object poems is first a short narrative of discovery. How did this object come into the poet's vision? Next follows an observation of the object. What does it look like, smell like, feel like, taste like? Then comes the fantasy: where does the object take the poet in his imagination? This is the leap—from the conscious to the unconscious. "One's task," continues Bly, "is not only to snap the picture but to develop it in a darkroom." The poet takes the image into the dark, into the unknown. And finally he brings it back, now seen in a new way.

Let's look at one of Bly's object poems, published in *The Prose Poem*, Volume 3, to see how he does this.

"THE PINE CONE"

This pine cone, about eight inches long, looks like a trunk that never developed a head. The cone trunk holds out silent and stiffened arms.

When we lift it to the nose, the odor suggests country bars, arguments in parking lots, dwarves who have invented a fuel.

But if the tongue reaches out, sap coats the curly tongue; the lips stick to each other. We feel the difficulty in getting free from silences . . . the hired man in the spare room . . . what happened that spring. Don't bother. Our whole family is like that.

A pine cone. Bly describes what it looks like in the first paragraph. The images are strong: a trunk without a head but with silent and stiffened arms. Then the odor takes him to the second paragraph. Fantasy: country bars, arguments, dwarves who have invented a fuel. A strange smell. Now the touch takes the reader to the third paragraph. Your lips stick to each other. And fantasy: the hired man, what happened last spring (ellipses are the poet's). And finally Bly brings you back to reality, the metaphor of the pine cone is his whole family, without a head, silent arms, silences that stick to lips.

The first time I worked with object poems was in the class of the poet, Myra Shapiro. She explained how Robert Bly taught this type of poem. He said that the pattern would be from observation (of the object), to fantasy, to discovery. She asked that we bring to class some object from nature that called to us, and that we write about it.

On my way to class the next day, I plucked a tiny yellow cinquefoil flower from a bush along my path. It is a flower that also grows near my house in Switzerland. In class I held the five-petaled flower in my hand and looked at it. I felt it, I tasted it, I listened to it. Then I wrote a few sentences describing it.

Next Shapiro suggested we skip to our fathers. "Make a leap and write about your father." My father had died ten years earlier. I remembered going to the memorial service. As I held the cinquefoil in my hand, I felt how light it was and this took me to the lightness of my father's ashes. So I wrote about that.

Now we were told to bring the two paragraphs together, discover a link. I kept holding the cinquefoil in my hand, realizing that I had never held my father's ashes. Yet how deeply I felt his roots. I wrote about that, and here is the prose poem. Not as I wrote it that first day, but after much polishing.

"Cinquefoil"

I hold in the palm of my hand a tiny yellow flower, a cinquefoil. The five petals form a mandala around the inner circle of seeds. The seeds are dark. The stem is hidden. My gaze is drawn to the center then out again to each petal. The flower weighs nothing, as light as air. When I close my eyes, I no longer know whether it is in my hand or has fallen to the ground.

My father's ashes were as light as air, scattered in the small courtyard. I could not hold them in my hand. They were scattered before my arrival. I entered the church and wept. The long stem of grief stretched through me. My father in each tear. His melanoma surrounded by moist earth. Tumor spots dark brown like seeds.

The stem is slender and pulls me to the ground. My father always said, "Go do it." But now the doing is toppling me over. The flower needs to rest its head. The petals curl and shrivel. My father's ashes are light, light as my yellow flower. But his seeds are planted deep.

The pattern of the three paragraphs is evident. First I describe the flower. Then I move to my father's death, letting the images echo the description of the flower. In the third paragraph I pull the two subjects together, the flower becoming a metaphor for myself.

It's your turn to write an object prose poem, from observation to leap to recognition. I'd like to suggest that you go for a short walk inside or outside your home and find an object in your surroundings that you can hold in your hand. A pine cone, a stone, a flower. Hold it gently, look at it, touch it, smell it, listen to it, lick it if you will. Slowly start to write about it. Describe it. Observe it. Then close your eyes and make a leap, from the object to a fantasy. Where does it take you? If you need a suggestion, make a leap to someone you love. Surprise yourself. Keep writing. Now bring yourself—and the reader—back to reality with a last sentence.

✎ Exercise: Start to write an object prose poem. Ten minutes.

Find time later to polish your prose poem, to look for the elements of poetic prose—rhythm, imagery, compression, paradox—and heighten (deepen) the written expression. For now, give your prose poem a title. This is an object prose poem to place alongside your narrative prose poem: two short surprises of poetic prose.

✎ In this lesson, there are two short five-minute exercises (writing a sentence in meter, writing word sounds), two ten-minute exercises (writing a short paragraph with attention first to rhythm, then to imagery), and then another two ten-minute ones (starting a narrative prose poem and an object prose poem). If you do the lesson over a period of a month, I suggest that you do the first two during the first week, the second two during the second week, and then the last two during the third and fourth week.

The Alchemy
of Imagination

In *The Writing Life,* Annie Dillard describes the line of words as a miner's pick. It's time to take the pick and dig deeper to mine the gold. As you did in Lesson Five, you will tap further into your creativity. There, you worked with dreams. In this lesson, you will work with alchemy, an ancient way of transforming ordinary metals into gold, of turning the ordinary into the extraordinary, of finding the sparks of creativity within.

Alchemy: the word sounds foreign—and with reason. It comes from the Greek *chemeia,* derived from *Khem,* an ancient name for Egypt, and the Arabic definite article *al.* Hence, its roots are Egyptian, Arabic, and Greek. The earliest existing alchemical texts are papyri in Greek describing a mysterious art that originated in Egypt.

What is this ancient art? Marie-Louise von Franz, a colleague of C.G. Jung, defines it as a natural science that attempts to understand the mystery of nature. On the chemical side, it searches for the philosopher's stone, the substance that transmutes base metals into gold. On the spiritual side, for the elixir (*al-iksir* in Arabic) of immortality, the sparks of the Creator within the creation. And on the psychological side for the Self, the archetype of fullness, the pattern of wholeness.

I ask you to become an alchemist during this lesson as you find living images in your dreams, memories, and surroundings and follow them into the dark, into the unknown. You will listen to these images, writing dialogues. Then you will shape and polish the nuggets of gold that you have unearthed and brought into the light—writing journal entries, essays, short stories, or poems.

THE HISTORY OF ALCHEMY

First, by way of an introduction, here is a short history of alchemy, starting with one of the oldest known texts: "The Prophetess Isis to her Son," copied into a Greek manuscript dating from the first century our era. Marie-Louise von Franz gives this account in her book, *Alchemy:* When one of the angels wanted to make love to Isis, she asked him first for the alchemical secret of making gold. The angel said it was beyond his knowledge and sent a greater angel. The greater angel also wanted to make love to Isis. He did give her the secret; it is not known if they made love. The antique recipe for the elixir of alchemy begins, "Take quicksilver, fix it in lumps of earth or by magnesia or sulphur and retain it. Take one part of lead and of the preparation fixed through warmth, and two parts of white stone . . ." The recipe continues, growing more and more complex.

Aristotle believed that all things tend toward perfection. Since gold is the most perfect metal, it was reasonable to believe that nature created it out of other metals hidden deep within the earth. Echoing the recipe from the Prophetess Isis, Aristotle gave instructions to whiten the earth, sublime it with fire, until the Spirit within was released. He defined the whitened earth as "quintessence."

In China there is the ancient alchemical text, *The Secret of the Golden Flower,* dating from the ninth century but containing much earlier Taoist and Buddhist ideas. It is a manual of meditation used by students of spiritual masters that uncovers the way—through practice and steadfastness—to find immortality, to create the golden flower, the golden elixir of life.

In the early dark ages, alchemical texts abound in Arabia with Mohammed ibn Umail, and six centuries later in Europe with the Swiss physician and alchemist Paracelsus and his disciple Dorn, the first Western alchemist to recognize that the elixir of immortality could be found by reading and meditating.

Today, following the insights of C.G. Jung, who studied deeply the ancient alchemical texts, scholars and artists continue to delve into the obscurities of alchemy, to find the path through darkness to light. All these traditions speak to the same purpose: to find the sparks of light—the seeds of creativity—that are hidden in the physical world. As a writer, you can walk along the path of alchemy, following an image into the dark, distilling it, and then bringing it back to the light. But instead of transforming lumps of earth and quicksilver, you will work to transform your writing.

FINDING LIVING IMAGES

In order to write your way through alchemy, it is necessary to find living images—the images that open doors to the invisible. These are the images that will lead you deeper into the unknown where you can work as an alchemist. Rainer Maria Rilke wrote in *Letters to a Young Poet* that first you must go within, and then you must "use to express yourself the things in your environment, the images from your dreams, the objects of your memory." You will look at each of these sources—dreams, memories, surroundings—reading examples from other writers in order to discover your own.

DREAMS

Throughout history, dreams have been recorded and listened to as humankind sought to understand the language of their gods. If you wish, you may return to the detailed summary of the history of dreams in Lesson Five. From ancient times, dreams have revealed another dimension to human life. By 3000 B.C.E., in Memphis, Egypt, there were dream temples where people would go to share their dreams with "doctors" who would interpret them.

Skipping to the twentieth century, Freud's *Interpretation of Dreams* explored the unconscious background of human consciousness, calling dreams "the royal road to the unconscious." Jung explored a still deeper level of the unconscious, referring to it as the "collective unconscious," our common heritage of myths, folklore, and art. It is our dreams—those little hidden doors in the recesses of our psyches—that open the way.

Think back and remember one of your dreams, then follow it into the unknown to find a living image. In my book, *Looking for Gold*, each chapter begins with a dream. Here is one example.

"Pieces of Gold"

It is night time. I am going through a moonlit yard, around
a large mansion with lights in the windows. I go inside
and find myself in a small room with Pierre, looking at
gold jewelry that is mine. A dark figure is behind us,
watching. At first we think he is there to admire the gold.
Then we realize he wants to steal the jewelry. Pierre leaves
me and I put the pieces safely away. The dark figure is still
in the room. . . .

That is my dream. Now how can this dream be a door into the
unknown? Following the steps of dream-work from Lesson
Five, first remember the dream. Write it down—even just a
few lines in the middle of the night, and then more at length
during the day. Second, note your feelings about the dream. I
liked the moonlit yard, the mansion with lighted windows. I
liked the gold. The third step is to work with associations.
What association can you make with your life? The dream took
me back to a book I had just read about alchemy. The fourth
step is to work with amplification, dipping into the collective
unconscious. Here the dream led me to see the thief-like figure
as Hermes, the young god who stole Apollo's herds but who
was also the messenger of the gods. As the dream took me
deeper, I worked with the image of the dark figure, the trick-
ster. Was he coming to steal the jewelry, or to tell me I can't put
my pieces of gold away?

Here is another dream, the dream of the young shepherd boy
in *The Alchemist* by Paolo Coelho. Here Santiago relates his dream
to the old Gypsy woman whom he hopes will reveal to him its
meaning.

FROM *THE ALCHEMIST*

"I have had the same dream twice," he said. "I dreamed I was in a field with my sheep, when a child appeared and began to play with the animals . . ."

"Tell me more about your dream," said the woman.

"And suddenly, the child took me by both hands and transported me to the Egyptian pyramids."

He paused for a moment to see if the woman knew what the Egyptian pyramids were. But she said nothing.

"Then at the Eyptian pyramids, the child said to me, 'If you come here, you will find a hidden treasure.' And just as she was about to show me the exact location, I woke up. Both times."

Santiago is spellbound by his dream. The Gypsy woman at first is silent. She will finally tell him that the dream will lead him across the desert to the Pyramids in Egypt. There he will find the treasure.

Now write one of your dreams. Close your eyes for a moment. What dream comes to you, from last night, last week, or from long ago? Write it down; free-write. Do not worry about words. Let your hand remember the dream.

✎ Exercise: Write one of your dreams. Five minutes.

Stop writing and read what you have written. What image resonates? What image leads you deeper—the pieces of gold, the thief, the sheep, the child, the Egyptian pyramids? Circle the image that speaks to you. Remember that you are looking for images to take you into the unknown and to unfold your stories.

✎ Exercise: Read your dream and circle an image. A few
   minutes.

MEMORIES

Memories are a second source of living images. Memory is everything you've lived up to the present moment. Each person you
meet, each place you visit, each event in your life dwells within
you. What memories call to you—a recent experience, a past
experience? Rilke continues in the same first letter to a young
poet, "Even if you were in some prison the walls of which let
none of the sounds of the world come to your senses—would you
not then still have your childhood, that treasure chest of memories?" Find a childhood memory that wants to come to light.

   Look at how a contemporary author writes from memories.
Here is a paragraph from Eva Hoffman's *Lost in Translation: A
Life in a New Language,* where she is remembering her childhood in Cracow before her parents took her to Vancouver when
she was thirteen.

FROM *LOST IN TRANSLATION*, "PARADISE"

I've snuggled under an enormous goose feather quilt covered
in hand-embroidered silk. Across the room from me is my
sister's crib. From the front room I hear my parents' breathing.
The maid—one of a succession of country girls who come to
work for us—is sleeping in the kitchen. It is Cracow 1949. I'm
four years old and I don't know that this happiness is taking
place in a country recently destroyed by war. . . . I only know
that I'm in my room which to me is everything, and that the
patterns on the ceiling are enough to fill me with a feeling of
sufficiency.

In writing this memory of her childhood, Hoffman has created for the reader a scene of security and happiness, as the child snuggles under a goose feather quilt while the rest of the household sleeps. Her room is everything, and the patterns on the ceiling comfort her.

Here is Michael Ondaatje remembering his childhood in *Running in the Family,* the account of his journey back to Sri Lanka. In one short memory, he gives life not only to dark squadrons of bats, but also to beautiful girls and to his parents listening to the cricket scores.

From "Monsoon Notebook (ii)"

The bars across the windows did not always work. When bats would invade the house at dusk, the beautiful long-haired girls would rush to the corner of rooms and hide their heads under dresses. The bats suddenly drifting like dark squadrons through the house—for never more than two minutes—arcing into the halls over the uncleared dining room table and out along the verandah where the parents would be sitting trying to capture the cricket scores on the BBC with a shortwave radio.

The vivid details make the reader see and feel the bats invading the house at dusk. How does Ondaatje remember the house? The bars across the window not working, the dining room table not cleared, and his parents sitting on the verandah trying to capture cricket scores. The memory sharpens as he remembers the visual details.

Now write one of your memories. Close your eyes. Go within. What memory wants to be written about? Go back to your childhood. Be quiet. When the memory calls to you, write it down. Without thinking, without stopping. Let it take you where it will.

✎ Exercise: Write down a memory. Five minutes.

After five minutes, stop writing and read your memory. As you did with the dream that you wrote earlier in this lesson, ask yourself what image resonates. What image, what detail, carries with it strong emotions, a cluster of feelings? Circle the image that speaks to you.

✎ Exercise: Read your memory and circle an image. A few minutes.

SURROUNDINGS

Surroundings are a third source of images. Look at your surroundings—inside and outside your home. What images call to you? Imagine taking a walk through your house. Close your eyes. Open the front door—maybe the door itself resonates to you—and look around. The hallway, the kitchen table, the oriental rug in the living room, the large picture window. The glass bowl, the pewter plate. Go slowly. Look carefully. This is the setting of your life. What speaks to you?

Keeping your eyes closed, imagine you are going outside. Walk into the backyard, look at the fruit tree, the apple blossoms, the fragile pink center of a single blossom. Continue into the woods: the dark shadows, the play of sunlight filtering through the foliage. Keep walking: the ivy twisting around the tree trunks, the pebbles on the path, the sound they make under your shoes. What image calls to you?

Here is the story of an image that I continue to write about, an earthenware water jug that sits on the old wooden table in my kitchen.

FROM *LOOKING FOR GOLD:*

I was coming down from the Voirons, from the monastery where I had gone for a day of prayer when a bee flew into the car. Instead of stopping, I tried to kill it and drove right into a cliff. I turned over twice and pulled myself out of the wreck, picking up the water jug I bought at the monastery—an earthenware jug, pottery which the sister made—wrapped in one sheet of newspaper. An ambulance carried me to the hospital in Geneva. I was not hurt nor was the jug.

Then with time a crack started to appear on the jug, a fine line etching its way onto the smooth gray surface. I wrote a story about the water jug, how the crack was within it, making the jug vulnerable.

The jug greets me every morning when I enter the kitchen. I look at it and see the crack working its way upward. The jug is vulnerable. So am I. The crack still speaks to me.

Think back to other images that we have seen in different surroundings. Nina Burghild Holzer writes in her journal about the hawk waiting for the sun: "his head was facing east." Ettie Hillesum in *An Interrupted Life* writes about the lopped-off trees outside her window, "like emaciated ascetics." Barbara Kingsolver starts her essay "Life Is Precious, Or It's Not" writing about columbines that she now wants to plant everywhere "to make sure we remember." Robert Bly writes about a pine cone that looks like a trunk that never developed a head and holds out "silent and stiffened arms."

It is your turn to find an image in your surroundings or rather to let the image find you. Close your eyes, go back to the walk you took inside or outside your home. What image calls to you? Take your time. When the image is there, hold it in your imagination and then describe it. Let it take you where it wants.

✎ Exercise: Describe an image in your surroundings. Five minutes.

FOLLOWING THE IMAGE INTO THE UNKNOWN

You will now become an alchemist. You will let the image lead you into the unknown. This is the first step of alchemy, the burning away of what is not essential; it is called *nigredo* (darkening). While you cannot put your image into an alchemical vase and heat it in a furnace, you can work with it this way in your imagination. C.G. Jung called this "active imagination," comparing it to conscious daydreaming. You empty your mind and then through active imagining—holding on to the image, seeing it on the stage, taking part in the play—you let the image reveal its meaning.

First, choose just one image. You have found three images—one from your dream, one from a memory of childhood, and one from your surroundings. Which one now resonates the most? This will be the image that you will follow into the dark. Close your eyes and take your time. When the image has found you, write it down, in a few words.

✎ Exercise: Choose one of your images and describe it.
Five minutes.

Now hold on to it, give it your special attention, and let it lead you into the dark. To help you do this, there is an exercise I call "Drawing a Meander." You will draw a path following your image into the unknown. This path itself is the meander of an imaginary river from one side of the paper to the other. We used to think that meanders had no direction. But we now realize that underlying the seemingly erratic course of a river, there is a pattern. Try to let your unconscious guide you to an underlying pattern.

To begin, place your paper horizontally and write the name of your image on the far left side. Then, half closing your eyes, let your hand draw a meander—a winding path—from the image across the page. This is the path you will follow with your words. For example, if I do this with the image of my water jug, I note the jug to the left and trace, with my eyes half shut, a meandering path across the paper. I then open my eyes, look at my meander, and begin to jot down brief notes about my jug along the way. The path will illuminate my story.

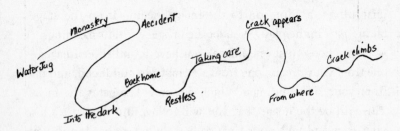

The Meander of My Water Jug

At the beginning of the meander, the path goes upward. I remember crashing into the stone cliff. I note this in a few words.

The meander then drops. I faint and enter the dark. I continue to write down words as I go home with my jug. The path goes up and down. I am restless. But slowly it rises. The crack appears and the meander drops again. I wonder where the crack comes from. The meander starts to climb again. I note that the crack starts to climb. And I start to climb. My meander is revealing the lesson of my water jug.

Before drawing your own meander, read at how Terry Tempest Williams lets herself follow the image of a flash flood. This excerpt is from the chapter "Labor" in her book *Red: Passion and Patience in the Desert*.

From "Labor" in *Red*

The wall of water hits. Waves turn me upside down and sideways as I am carried downriver, tumbling in the current, dizzy in the current, dark underwater, holding my breath, holding my breath. I cannot see but believe I will surface, believe I will surface, holding my breath. The muscle of the river is pushing me down, deeper and deeper, darker and darker. I cannot breathe, I am dying under the pressure, the pressure creates change, a change of heart. The river changes its heart and pushes me upward with the force of a geyser. I surface, I breathe. I am back in the current, moving with the current, floating in the current, face up, on my back. There are others around me, our silt-covered bodies navigating downriver, feet pointing downriver. We are part of the river . . .

Williams submerges herself in the wall of water. Tumbling in the current, she goes under deeper and deeper until the river changes its heart. She surfaces, floating in the current. She becomes part of the river.

Now it's your turn to draw a meander. Take your piece of paper and note your image to the left, the starting point of your meander. Close your eyes for a moment, then with eyes half shut, let your hand draw a meander across the paper. Do not direct it. Let it flow from within, in the semi-darkness. Once you're done, look at your meander. Go back to your image and note its story. Let it lead you along your meander. Where does it take you? Upward? Down into the dark? Jot down notes. What happens to it? What happens to you? Let yourself be surprised.

✎ Exercise: Draw a meander, then add notes along the
    way where the image is taking you. Ten minutes.

Give your meander a title. Note the date and the place. By noting the time and setting, you are able to monitor yourself and learn when and where you write most freely.

LISTENING TO THE IMAGE

Albedo, the second step of alchemy, is the washing and distilling. The whitening. After the first step, the darkening, *nigredo,* comes the lightening, *albedo.* Where did the image take you? What did it reveal to you? You are looking for the symbolic significance of the image. What has it uncovered in your unconscious? What is my water jug telling me? I have written about this several times, each time reaching deeper into my unconscious, discovering new meaning.

To help find the meaning of your image, talk to it, listen to it. This is another way to practice active imagination: writing dialogues with your images. Imagine questioning your image. Imagine your image questioning you. Here is another short excerpt from Paolo Coehlo's *The Alchemist*. The shepherd boy Santiago is speaking to the wind that he has encountered in the desert. He wants the wind to help him return to his loved one out over the sands.

FROM *THE ALCHEMIST*

"Help me," the boy said. "One day you carried the voice of my loved one to me."

"Who taught you to speak the language of the desert and the wind?"

"My heart," the boy answered . . .

"You can't be the wind," the wind said. "We're two very different things."

"That's not true. I learned the alchemist's secrets in my travels. I have inside me the winds, the deserts, the stars, and everything created in the universe."

As Santiago and the wind question one another, they mutually inform each other. Imagine speaking to your image. Ask a question. Listen to the response. Write down the dialogue. You could start with the question, "Why are you here?" or "What do you want to tell me?" You are asking your image. Then you let your image answer. Perhaps it will ask you a question. Remember you are looking for meaning. This is the second step of alchemy. You are distilling.

✎ Exercise: Write a dialogue with your image. Ten minutes.

GIVING WRITTEN EXPRESSION TO THE IMAGE
AND POLISHING

After black *(nigredo)* and white *(albedo),* comes red, *rubedo.* Rubedo is the third step of alchemy: the reddening, the new consciousness. This is the polishing that turns your images into pieces of gold. This is the crafting and fine tuning of a journal entry, an essay, a short story, a poem.

Here, for example, is a short prose poem, written from the experience of following my water jug into the dark.

"The Crack"

In the monastery, the little sister turned the earthenware jug, one ring at a time. She turned the jug in silence, shaping the long spiral of clay into ever smaller circles as she neared the top. Hands cupped in prayer, she smoothed the still moist surface.

Only later did the crack appear. It climbs upward through the rings of clay. Like a fine vein, it etches itself into the surface, coming from deep within, from the silence of its creator.

A prose poem about the crack, a bit of rubedo found in the story of my water jug. The polishing and the deepening of the image. A new awareness. The crack comes from within the jug, from within its maker.

Here is another example of rubedo from Terry Tempest Williams' book, *Red.* After imagining the flash flood, she is walking in the desert. This is her journal entry. And it is worthwhile to note that this is all there is on the page in her book. The entry is centered in the middle of the page. Around it is white space, inviting the reader to enter and rest for a moment.

"ENTRY"

Redstone. Heartstone. Blood red in the company of green.
See how much passionate life stands out even in this endless
expanse of desert. A redstone in the sand. Simply that. It
brought my body down, inspired my hand to hold one small
stone. I believe in the fire of an idea.

—Journal entry,
September 8, 2000

A redstone in the sand. It called to her, it brought her body
down. She bent over and picked up one small stone. She held in
her hand the fire of an idea. Heartstone. And she wrote it down
in her journal.

Now it's your turn to give a written expression to an image. This
can be a journal entry or a short prose poem. It can be a memory, a
dream, or a dialogue, as Coehlo did in *The Alchemist*. Write slowly.
Craft this fragment as you would polish a piece of gold.

✎ Exercise: Give a written expression to your image. Ten
minutes.

When you have finished, or when the ten minutes have passed,
close your eyes and find a title for your writing. This is your
piece of gold, found along the meander of your imagination
while you worked as an alchemist. In the days ahead, find time
to polish it.

✎ This lesson has four short exercises (writing a dream, a
memory, and a surrounding, and describing an image that resonates) and three longer ones (drawing a meander, writing a dialogue, and crafting a piece of writing). You may follow the

suggested time spans, or you may work with the lesson over the course of a month. In that case, I suggest that you do the first three exercises during the first week, then the second week do the fourth short exercise, along with the exercise of the meander. The remaining two longer exercises would follow, one week each.

Mosaics and Memoir

In this last stretch of one year to a writing life, we tackle longer works of writing. As Eduardo Galeano said about his books, we will start with fragments—short pieces that begin to integrate themselves into a whole. We will make mosaics, whether writing novels or memoirs. Regardless of what genre you choose, the way of a mosaic applies to both fiction and non-fiction. All year you have been writing fragments—in fiction: short stories, short-shorts, contemporary tales, dialogues; in nonfiction: journal entries, personal essays, op-eds, travel essays, and dialogues. And dreams: are they fiction or nonfiction? And prose poetry? Is it prose or poetry? Is it fiction or nonfiction? This is where definitions, categories, labels all fall short. As the memoir leads down many roads and includes different forms of writing, I will focus on this form here. But remember that a writing life is a life that writes in any genre.

THE WAY OF A MOSAIC

Mosaic is defined in *Merriam-Webster's New Collegiate Dictionary* as "a decoration made by inlaying small pieces of variously colored material to form pictures and patterns." In writing works of prose as mosaic, the writer assembles the pieces of memory as he would the pieces of a mosaic. You look for the various colors and shapes. You move them around to find different patterns. You form pictures of your life with them. You write this way by accumulation and association.

At an Authors Guild Symposium, Frank McCourt said that during the years that he was encouraging his students to write about themselves and their families, his own book began to coalesce. He had tried to write a version thirty years earlier and qualified it as appalling. Then, McCourt explained, a personal voice appeared. "A child began to speak. I had a lot of stuff in notebooks and I reverted to the notebooks and it was a mosaic approach . . . I just put the pieces together." A personal voice and a mosaic approach came together in writing his memoir *Angela's Ashes*.

Let's look at a few books, both fiction and nonfiction, that were written in the form of a mosaic. First one that is both: *The Way Forward Is with a Broken Heart* by Alice Walker. The book begins with a story, "merging fact with fiction," Walker explains. It is her version of the life she lived with her husband of a different culture and race in the violent Deep South state of Mississippi. She then goes on to imagine stories that grew out of the life that followed that marriage. Stories that are mostly fiction but have come out of her life.

In *Running in the Family* by Michael Ontdaatje, which we looked at in the last lesson. Ondaatje begins with a dream: he is already in the jungle in Sri Lanka looking for the traces of his parents. By linking travelogues, personal essays, conversations, poems, memories, and even a chapter of graffiti copied from the walls of ancient caves, Ondaatje assembles a heartwarming mosaic not only of Sri Lanka forty years ago and his parents, but also of himself.

Like Water for Chocolate: A Novel in Monthly Installments with Recipes, Romances and Home Remedies, by Laura Esquivel, is a work of fiction written as mosaic. The book is divided into twelve sections named after the months of the year. Each starts with a recipe from the protagonist Tita's memory and imagination. It describes how the dish is prepared and links it to an event in Tita's life. Esquivel has placed the recipes to the side of the page, illustrating the mosaic approach to her novel.

For the Time Being is a work of nonfiction in which Annie Dillard weaves together a natural history of sand, a catalog of clouds, statistics about newborn babies, the story of Teilhard de Chardin, a trip to Jerusalem, and a series of encounters. Dillard is trying to make sense of life's mysteries. In the author's note, she writes that gradually the different scenes, true stories, facts, and ideas will grow familiar and that together they will present a complex picture of the world today as she sees it.

Likewise, in *Negotiating with the Dead,* Margaret Atwood writes that her nonfiction book inherited its shape from its progenitors. The grab bag nature of the citations reflects the inside of her head. She explains that the organization of the chapters is not sequential; one chapter does not lead directly into the next. However, they all circle around a set of common themes—the writer, her medium, and her art.

There are many more examples of both fiction and nonfiction written as mosaic. In fiction, think of *Soul Mountain* by the Nobel Prize winner Gao Xingjian (written from three different points of view, weaving together stories from ancient Chinese history, folk tales, childhood reminiscences, memories of the Cultural Revolution, and portraits of fellow wanderers). Think of *Fugitive Pieces* by Anne Michaels (interlocking the stories of two men from different generations, bridging present and past with poetry, botany, and art). And *Girl in Hyacinth Blue* by Susan Vreeland (eight connected stories revolving around a single painting by Vermeer and moving backward in time).

In nonfiction, think of *Leap* by Terry Tempest Williams (an innovative hybrid, woven of memories, dreams, lived experience, reflections, all revolving around Hieronymus Bosch's triptych "The Garden of Delights"). Think of *The Color of Water* by James McBride, alternating the voice of his mother and his own, juxtaposing the two stories. And Kathleen Norris' *The Cloister Walk,* written with journal entries of one liturgical year and short prose pieces about celibacy, music, and religion, back to back with meditations.

Whether you work with the form of a mosaic in a novel or in a memoir, it is a way to gather the different pieces of writing into a comprehensive whole. As you look to writing longer works, remember that writers are readers. Remember Amy Clampitt, who said the one thing writers need are predecessors. Read! We learn from Annie Dillard, Margaret Atwood, Gao Xingjian, Kathleen Norris, and so many other excellent writers waiting to be discovered and shared. Francine Prose, in her book *Reading Like a Writer,* says "In the ongoing process of becoming a writer, I read and re-read the authors I most loved."

Now before we proceed to look more closely at a few examples of mosaic-like memoirs, let's review the memoir itself. What is it? How does it work?

INTRODUCTION TO MEMOIR

The memoirist explores a subject in order to define a self and a world, shaping life experience into story, into personal myth. Jung asked, "What is your myth—the myth in which you live?" What is your world view? How does your life fit into it? In short, what is the meaning of your life? A memoirist recounts a life experience and tries to make meaning out of it.

In the contemporary world, there is a need to testify, an urgency to share real-life stories and to learn from one another. It is through memoir—writing memoir and reading memoir— that we discover our connectedness, our oneness with another, our common humanity. Each time you discover meaning in your life, you contribute to the greater meaning of human life. From your daily individual life, you touch the eternal, universal life.

The first western memoirist was Saint Augustine. In his *Confessions,* written in 397, he used memory to provide access to his deeper self and the Divine. "Now I arrive in the fields and vast mansions of memory, where are treasured innumerable images brought in there from objects of every conceivable kind perceived by the senses." It is in these mansions of memory that Augustine comes to meet himself and to climb to his Creator. "See I am climbing through my mind to you who abide high above me." It was not his life history that he was writing, but rather a life narrative in which his search for God is the driving force.

Here is the difference between autobiography and memoir. Autobiography is one's life history, as biography is the life history of someone else. Memoir, however, is a window into one's life. The writer chooses the lens. St. Augustine chooses his lens—his search for God—and selects the memories that furthered his search. He starts with his childhood, looking back for the places where his God might be found. What are the memories that will lead him to an understanding of his Divinity? In sharing his selected memories, St. Augustine shares his focus, enlightening his readers, enlightening humankind.

The essence of memoir, then, is the writer's search for meaning and the reader's response. The memoirist speaks to the reader as to a friend, creating a space where she and her reader come together. The reader wants to know how the memoirist makes sense of her life in order to do the same for his own life. Here is an excerpt from Maureen Murdock's recent book, *Unreliable Truth: On Memoir and Memory*.

FROM THE CHAPTER "MEMOIR AND MYTH"

Three summers ago, while on an early morning walk through the hay fields outside Lavigny, Switzerland, I met a woman walking her dog. We fell into step next to each other and she asked me if I was staying at the writers' residency. When I told her yes she asked me what I was writing. I tentatively mumbled something about memory and metaphor, hoping she wouldn't pursue the conversation. It's hard for me to discuss what I am writing about when I am in the middle of it. Instead, she immediately asked, "Do you know Joseph Campbell?" . . . And here I was at 7:00 am, discussing mythology with a Swiss economist from Bern who had learned about myth while working in India!

Because we have become such a mobile culture, living in many cases, across continents from our families and loved ones, we yearn for community, consciously or not. Reading a memoir or sitting in a memoir class listening to the lives of other people gives us a sense of perspective about our own life as well as a link to a community. If I write about some experience in my life and reflect on it in such a way that it touches

your experience of your life, then we have made connection .
. . something happens on a deep level to both of us.

Murdock shows here how memoir connects us to community.
But such connection is possible only when the memoirist is
remembering to the best of her ability and sincerely trying to
make sense of it. When we see titles like Murdock's *Unreliable
Truth,* or William Zinsser's *Inventing the Truth: The Art and
Craft of Memoir,* we are tempted to think that the memoirist can
invent the memory. No, the memoirist does not fabricate the
experience, nor does she fabricate the memory. But she does
relate the experience as only she remembers it. Another person
would remember the experience differently. Zinsser explains the
choice of his title, saying that when he was interviewing different memoirists, he realized that the writer of a memoir
becomes the editor of his or her own life, "imposing a narrative
pattern on a mass of half-remembered events." Hence, inventing
the truth. It is important to be very clear here. As I wrote in
Lesson Two, dealing with the personal essay, nonfiction writers
make every effort to come as close as they can to what they see
and feel. The pledge of the nonfiction writer is to write about
what happened, not to invent something that did not happen.

The transmission of a memory depends, then, upon its reality
but also upon the imagination of the memoirist. In order to be
read and appreciated, the memory has to be vibrant, it has to
resonate. The memoirist Patricia Hampl in her essay "The Need
to Say It" speaks of the inevitable tango of memory and imagination: "How uncanny to go back in memory to a house from
which time has stolen all the furniture and to find the one
remembered chair and write it so large, so deep, that it furnishes
the entire vacant room." We may remember only the one chair,

but we can imagine it—so large, so deep—that it fills the entire room, even the entire house. Memory and imagination hold hands in writing memoir.

In her memoir *Mother Tongue: An American Life in Italy,* poet Wallis Wilde-Menozzi addresses another element of memoir: the canvas against which the memoir is set. Menozzi writes that she cannot describe the experience of her life in Parma without including the life and history of her family and of the *Parmigiani* themselves. She writes from the center of her experience and offers the reader a view into the confrontation of cultures, but also into the beauty and lasting humanism of Italy. In the chapter "Bread," even the humble *micca,* Parma's bread, the size of a laborer's fist, links the past and the present—"served more than once a day in this way [it] echoes the mass, said morning and evening in many of the churches in the city."

The memoirist writes to find not only a self, but a world. Gabriel Garcia Márquez gives the readers of *Living to Tell the Tale* not only a memoir sumptuous in remembered scenes of his early life, but also a major work of national history. Márquez writes in the opening page, "Life is not what one lived, but what one remembers and how one remembers it in order to recount it."

Elie Wiesel's memoir *Night* is a terrifying record of his memories of the death of his family and the death of his own innocence, at Auschwitz and then at Buchenwald. Wiesel has transformed his anguish into art. In his preface, he writes that if he were to write only one book in his lifetime, it would be *Night*. Then he asks himself why he wrote it. To not go mad? Or rather to go mad in order to understand madness? To leave behind a legacy of words, of memories? Or simply to preserve a record of his survival? Then why his and not another's? Wiesel answers, "Having survived, I needed to give some meaning to my survival."

To give meaning to his experience. Here is the raison d'être of memoir.

EXAMPLES OF MEMOIR AS MOSAIC

Before starting your own mosaic, look at the following examples. In writing *Circling to the Center,* I wanted to focus on different chapters of my life—different moments—when I felt a strong call to silent prayer. But I did not want to start at birth and go through to old age. Instead the book took shape from a flower, my cinquefoil, that I wrote about in a prose poem (see page 157). I decided to write five chapters, one for each of the petals. I added legends from different spiritual traditions. I was working by accumulation and association. I included photographs and drawings, mandalas and monoprints. It was a mosaic.

Look at how Isabel Huggan has put together her memoir *Belonging.* It is written in segments, in the same way that poetry is written in stanzas. At the core is the old stone house, Mas Blanc, situated among vineyards in southern France. Here is a passage from the chapter "Fire," in which Huggan accumulates memories of fires and associates them to the four seasons, each one written as a different segment. This is a memory in the spring segment.

FROM THE SEGMENT "SPRING FIRE"
In one corner of the [olive] grove we are burning dead wood left from last autumn's clearing of bushes along the roadside, and we keep a small fire going, throwing freshly cut branches on the flames from time to time, relishing the glorious oily sizzle and crackle. The old wood gives off a sweet white smoke like steam, but the olive burns black and

greasy, and there's a roaring sound deep in the blaze that grows during the afternoon. It seems like something savage dwells in the heart of the fire and I think I'd better get water "just in case" . . .

After making my way through a tangle of brambles, I bend down at a riverbank lush with violets and wild narcissus and see myself reflected in the still water just before I dip the pail. I have the vivid impression of having done this before, if not in life, then in a dream. Hauling the water back through wild iris and blackthorn, I stop to look up at the poplars on the other bank, their new leaves glimmering pale copper against the blue sky. *I am part of this place.*

Huggan is braiding event and memory. We see clearly the call of myth. She is looking for meaning in her life in southern France, tracing her story back in time.

In Eduardo Galeano's *The Book of Embraces,* the mosaic approach is still more apparent. Here Galeano has put together parable, poetry, anecdote, dream, travelogue, political commentary, and autobiography, along with his own surreal drawings. In an interview in *Fourth Genre* (Fall 2001), Galeano explains, "Fragments, it's what I am writing now, to recover all the little pieces of disintegrated reality so that each little piece can express the whole universe from its smallness." He begins working with very brief texts that later integrate themselves in the way they want. "The books write themselves." We would all like this to happen. Here is one of his fragments.

"THE FIESTA"

The sun was gentle, the air clear, and the sky cloudless.

Buried in the sand, the clay pot steamed. As they went from ocean to mouth, the shrimp passed through the hands of Fernando, master of ceremonies, who bathed them in a holy water of salt, onions, and garlic.

There was good wine. Seated in a circle, we friends shared the wine and shrimp and the ocean that spread out free and luminous at our feet.

As it took place, that happiness was already being remembered by our memory. It would never end, nor would we. For we are all mortal until the first kiss and the second glass, which is something everyone knows, no matter how small his or her knowledge.

From a memory of a picnic on the beach, of friends sharing wine and shrimp, Galeano has written a scene that lingers in the reader's mind and imagination. Each of his fragments is written on a new page, giving space for the reader to enter into this strange, allegorical world. Galeano explains in the same interview that while he writes about things that happened, sometimes it seems like fiction. "Because reality continues at night when it sleeps, or pretends to be sleeping, and then reality has a capacity for delirium, for magic. . ."

And now it's your turn. If you are already working on a memoir, use the following exercises to clarify your work and move it forward. If you are just beginning a memoir, please go slowly with each exercise. And no matter where you are in your writing, remember Rilke's words: "Everything is gestation and then bringing forth." Take your time. Enjoy the challenge. Discover your own story—the myth that you are living.

STARTING A MEMOIR
A Window into a Life

We have said that memoir is a window into our life. Just as

a house has many windows, so do our lives. We can write many memoirs. I have written about dreamwork, about prayer, about raising children in Europe. These are three windows. There are still many more. What is important is to find which window you want to write about. What are you passionate about? Joseph Campbell would ask, What is your bliss? What part of your life is calling to you for self-reflection? Think about this deeply. What will be the subject of your memoir?

If you are already working on a memoir, move to the exercise just below.

If you are just beginning, go back in your memory, or your journal pages, to what you have written in the past nine months while reading this book. Read your journal entries, your dreams, your personal essays, your prose poems. What images, what stories, resonate for you? Be the alchemist. Find the gold within yourself that you want to write about in a memoir. Take your time, then turn to this short exercise.

✎ Exercise: Write a few sentences about the window you wish to open into your life. Five minutes.

The Frame of the Window

Now just as a window has a frame, so does a memoir. What frame will you give to your memoir? How will you limit what you include? In her book *Writing the New Autobiography*, Tristine Rainer gives a list of possible limiting frames with examples. Here are some of them along with some of mine.

— A period in your life: Russell Baker's *Growing Up*, Maya Angelou's *I Know Why the Caged Bird Sings*

— A setting: Annie Dillard's *Pilgrim at Tinker Creek,* Jill Ker Conway's *The Road from Coorain*
— A particular theme (psychological, ecological, or spiritual): William Styron's *Darkness Visible,* Terry Tempest Williams' *Red: Passion and Patience in the Desert*
— Family: Patricia Hampl's *A Romantic Childhood,* Vivien Gornick's *Fierce Attachments*
— Language: *Alice Kaplan's French Lessons,* Wallis Wilde-Menozzi's *Mother Tongue*
— Reflections: C.G. Jung's *Memories, Dreams, Reflections,* Ettie Hillesum's *An Interrupted Life*
— Travel: Paul Theroux's *The Great Railway Bazaar,* W.S. Merwin's *Summer Doorways*
— Journals: Burghild Nina Holzer's *A Walk between Heaven and Earth,* May Sarton's *Journal of a Solitude*
— Collections: Alice Walker's *Anything We Love Can Be Saved,* Barbara Kingsolver's, *Small Wonder*

Imagine your window; what frame does it have? A period in your life? A place? A theme? A series of reflections? A voyage? A family history? A collection?

Look at Joan Didion's *The Year of Magical Thinking.* The window (the subject) is the sudden death of her husband John Gregory Dunne the night before New Year's Eve, 2003. It is her attempt to make sense of the weeks and months after "life changes in the instant." The book moves back and forth from memory to reflection. The frame is one year. This is the structure that lets Didion explore a marriage and a life, in good times and bad.

✎ Exercise: Write a few sentences about the frame of your window, the frame of your memoir. Five minutes.

The Parts to Include and the Parts to Exclude

Annie Dillard's essay "To Fashion a Text," included in Zinsser's book *Inventing the Truth,* states that the writer of any work, and particularly any nonfiction work, must decide what to put in and what to leave out. When she was writing *An American Childhood,* she asked herself the question, What am I writing about? It was about the passion of childhood. It was about a child's interior life and growing awareness of the world. So she went back in memories to her personal childhood, about her relationship to nature, her world in and around Pittsburgh, her parents. And she left out social history, the summer in Wyoming, her adventures with various young men, and anything that might trouble her family. This was her decision.

This brings up another important point. When you are writing nonfiction, are you careful about the people close to you? Do you show your work to the people whom you are writing about? This is each writer's decision. Dillard has answered this question. She leaves out anything that might trouble her family. And she offers to show her work to those people about whom she is writing.

Think now about what stories fit into your frame. Think dreams, memories, experiences, and reflections. Think also about the different forms of writing you can include: journal entries, personal essays, travelogues, dialogues, prose poems, fragments. Add photos, drawings. Kathleen Norris has included several weather reports in her memoir Dakota. In his memoir about his father, The Invention of Solitude, Paul

Auster gives the reader an amazingly lively portrait of his father through a list:

> From *The Invention of Solitude*
> The size of his hands. Their calluses.
> Eating the skin off the top of hot chocolate.
> Tea with lemon.
> The pairs of black, horn-rimmed glasses scattered through the house: on kitchen counters, on table tops, at the edge of the bathroom sink—always open, lying there like some strange, unclassified form of animal.
> Watching him play tennis.
> The way his knees sometimes buckled when he walked.
> His face.
> His resemblance to Abraham Lincoln, and how people always remarked on it.
> His fearlessness with dogs.
> His face. And again, his face.
> Tropical fish.

Even though his father was an intensely private, solitary person, Auster, in giving this list to the reader, has given life to his father. The reader sees him, feels he knows him.

Think lists. Be creative. Imagine all the different parts you can include. Don't shy away from something original. Include it.

Now think about the parts that don't fit. Be tough with yourself. What are the parts that will go into another frame, another memoir? Even those stories that you think are your very best. If they do not fit into this frame, put them aside. Do not worry; you will be happier for this and ultimately you will find a place for them.

✎ Exercise: Make a list of the parts you will include and
the parts you will exclude. Five minutes.

The Pattern

There is one more element to think about: the pattern that
you will give to the different parts. W.S. Merwin in
Summer Doorways follows his first trip abroad in 1948,
when he would have the luck to discover, to glimpse, to
touch for a moment some "ancient measureless way of
living." His memoir moves from doorway to doorway.
Kathleen Norris patterns *The Cloister Walk* on the liturgical world of the Benedictine Monastery where she was
spending two terms. Certain segments of the book leave
the monastery as she did for family reunions, work, and
life at her home. Always the book returns to the monastery,
where for Norris everything comes together. Karen Armstrong, in writing *The Spiral Staircase: My Climb Out of
Darkness,* patterned her memoir on a spiral, moving from
"The Devil of the Stairs" to "To Turn Again." The last sentence sees her climbing upward: turning again, she hopes,
toward the light.

What pattern will you use to link the different parts of
your memoir together? Perhaps it will be the months of a
year. Perhaps it will be a city street. A market. Think of
colors: might there be a color linking together the memories? Think of a garden with its different plants, flowers,
and bushes. Think of a treasure chest: Are you finding one
memory at a time? Are memories circling around the same
one center? And leave room for surprise. A new pattern
may superimpose itself as you work on your memoir.

✎ Exercise: Write down what pattern you might use. Five
minutes.

IMAGINING THE MOSAIC

Now that you have found the window, defined the frame, listed
the parts, and looked for a pattern, you are ready to imagine the
mosaic. I suggest that first you draw it.

Take a piece of paper and draw a rectangle. This is the frame
of your mosaic. Once one of my students brought to class a felt
board on which she had placed the different parts of her memoir.
She had been in my class the year before and had worked with
the board and cutouts—each one a different color, a different
shape—all winter, moving the pieces around until she found
the design and composition she wanted for her memoir.

Remember, you are imagining a mosaic, a decoration made by
inlaying pieces of variously colored materials to make a picture.
Try it. Don't be linear. Think in images. Maybe use a pencil so
that you can erase and move the images around. Or better, use
Post-its; move them and play with them. Place the different
parts, the images, the memories, the stories, and see where they
belong.

✎ Exercise: Draw a rectangle for your mosaic and place the
different parts of your memoir in it. Fifteen minutes.

Now it is time to describe your memoir. If you are already
working on one, and have perhaps written several chapters,
then the exercise will be to imagine writing the introduction.
How would you present your memoir to the reader? What are
you sharing with your reader? What is important? Take the
reader's hand and lead him into your memoir.

If you are just beginning to think about writing a memoir, then the exercise will be a journal entry about the memoir you wish to write. What window into your life do you wish to write about? What is the subject? What will be the frame? What parts will you include? Be honest; go within. What pattern will link the different parts together? Remember May Sarton writing about getting down to the matrix. What do you really want to write about? What are some of the dark spots that you wish to look at more deeply?

✎ Exercise: Write a page, either as an introduction to a
    memoir you are writing or a journal entry about the
    memoir you wish to write. Ten minutes.

When you have both your drawing of a mosaic and your written description of your memoir—when you have thought and imagined and thought again—give your memoir a title. Write your name next to it. If you are in a workshop setting, you might each share your title, saying your name afterward. If you are alone, take a deep breath and read the title aloud, followed by your name. This will carry you forward and not let you back away. It is your way of honoring your commitment to your memoir, and to a writing life.

✎ The exercises may be done within the suggested time frame, or again spread out over a month. In this case, you could do the first two short exercises (the window and its frame) the first week, and the next two (the pattern and the parts) the second week. Then make your mosaic the third week, and write the introduction or the journal entry the fourth week.

Rewriting

Rewriting applies to every genre of writing, so it's fitting we should deal with this critical aspect in the final stretch of our year. Mark Twain said, "The difference between the right word and the nearly right word is the same as that between lightning and the lightning bug." In this workshop, we will go after the lightning.

When asked about rewriting, Ernest Hemingway said that he rewrote the ending to *A Farewell to Arms* thirty-nine times before he was satisfied. Vladimir Nabokov wrote that spontaneous eloquence seemed like a miracle and that he rewrote every word he ever published, and often several times. And Mark Strand, former poet laureate, says that each of his poems sometimes goes through forty to fifty drafts before it is finished. "I like rewriting and don't trust anything that comes spontaneously. It's just my way."

Rewriting means revising, re-vision, seeing anew. It does not mean editing. Editing comes after rewriting, once there is a revised piece that needs to be checked. This lesson offers a suggested checklist for rewriting that includes a list for editing at the end.

To follow this lesson, choose a piece of your writing to serve as a basis for rewriting throughout this chapter—an essay, a short story, a journal entry, a prose poem, or a page or so of a novel or a memoir. It should not be longer than two or three pages.

We will take one element of the checklist at a time to review your piece of writing in light of this particular aspect, using it as a laser beam to detect weak spots. Then we will rewrite and polish. Only then will we edit.

Remember what Hemingway, Nabokov, and Strand wrote about rewriting. Raymond Carver also rewrote, sometimes doing as many as twenty drafts of the same story. In *The Writer's Chapbook* edited by George Plimpton, Carver says that there is not much he likes better than to take a story and "work it over again." He urges the reader to remember great writers who rewrote almost endlessly, citing Tolstoy for one who was still making revisions on the galleys of *War and Peace*. This, he says, should encourage every writer.

So please enjoy this chapter. I too enjoy rewriting. Following is the checklist that you may use both for fiction and nonfiction and adapt for poetry. You will find the list repeated at the end of this lesson to use for easy reference.

CHECKLIST FOR REWRITING

1. Leads and Endings
— Does the first paragraph (first line) capture the reader's attention?
— Is the piece well framed? Does it begin too early, too late? End too early, too late?

— Are the lead and the ending compatible? Is there fore-shadowing?

— Is there a feeling of resolution (protagonist changes/ there is new meaning)?

— Is it closed or open-ended: wrapped up but still alive?

— Description (characterization and setting)

— Does each setting contribute to story?

— Show! Is description vivid, specific? Does it touch the senses?

— Are characters alive?

3. Dialogue

— Does the dialogue advance the characterization and story?

— Does it contribute to the tone?

— Is each character's voice unique?

4. Narrative Tug, Tension/Conflict

— Is there tension through opposites in settings, characters, dialogue?

— Is there a narrative tug, "profluence" (John Gardner)?

— Is the struggle worth the story?

5. Images, Similes, Metaphors, Symbols

— Are there central (controlling) images?

— Are there comparisons (similes/metaphors)?

— Are there deeper associations and substitutions (symbols)?

6. Genre and Shape, Whose Story, Point of View, Style, Rhythm, Voice

— Does the shape fit the story? Is the genre/subgenre right for the story?

— Whose story is it?

— In what point of view?

— Is the style appropriate to the subject (poetic, didactic, humorous)?

— Is the rhythm consistent (scanning for meter, word sounds, repetition)?

— Is author's voice full-bodied and consistent?

7. Theme and Meaning

— What is the subject (theme)?

— Is there clutter? Are the writer's ideas clear?

— Is there a moment of new awareness (Joyce's "epiphany")?

— Why is the story important?

Then, once the writing is revised:

8. Editing

— Title (Does it fit? Does it grab attention?)

— Length (too short/too long?)

— Sentences and paragraphs (varied/monotonous?)

— Verbs (active/passive? avoid verbs of being)

— Unnecessary words (adverbs, adjectives, clichés, complicated words, pet words, dialogue tags)

— Visual effect (placement of paragraphs, white space)

— Proofread for consistency, punctuation, spelling

TWO EXCERPTS

Here are two excerpts of prose, one fiction and one nonfiction, to illustrate the elements of the list. The first excerpt is the opening page of the novel *Sula* by Toni Morrison, where Morrison weaves a poetic spell on a setting and a community that disappear from the town of Medallion but remain in the reader's mind.

From *Sula*

In that place, where they tore the nightshade and blackberry patches from their roots to make room for the Medallion City

Golf Course, there was once a neighborhood. It stood in the hills above the valley town of Medallion and spread all the way to the river. It is called the suburbs now, but when black people lived there it was called the Bottom. One road, shaded by beeches, oaks, maples and chestnuts, connected it to the valley. The beeches are gone now, and so are the pear trees where children sat and yelled down through the blossoms to passersby . . .

There will be nothing left of the Bottom, but perhaps it is just as well, since it wasn't a town anyway: just a neighborhood where on quiet days people in valley houses could hear singing sometimes, banjos sometimes, and, if a valley man happened to have business up in those hills—collecting rent or insurance payments—he might see a dark woman in a flowered dress doing a bit of cakewalk, a bit of black bottom, a bit of "messing around" to the lively notes of a mouth organ. Her bare feet would raise the saffron dust that floated down on the coveralls and bunion-split shoes of the man breathing music in and out of his harmonica. The black people watching her would laugh and rub their knees, and it would be easy for the valley man to hear the laughter and not notice the adult pain that rested somewhere under the eyelids, somewhere under their head rags and soft felt hats, somewhere in the palm of the hand, somewhere behind the frayed lapels, somewhere in the sinew's curve . . .

For now, just appreciate the lush, carefully crafted writing. Listen to the lively notes of the mouth organ, watch the woman in the flowered dress doing a bit of cakewalk.

The second excerpt is the first page of Al Alvarez's memoir *Where Did It All Go Right?* The opening paragraphs set the tone for this fast-moving journey through a poet's and critic's life, where the focus is his love of poetry.

From Chapter One, "Provenance"

In 1938 my elder sister Anne came home from finishing school in Switzerland very upset by what was happening just across the border in Germany. One afternoon she persuaded my father to tune in to a short-wave broadcast of one of Hitler's Nuremberg rallies. The only short-wave radio was in my father's gramo-phone, a state-of-the-art, polished-walnut monster as big as a modern washing machine, but with a loudspeaker behind a fretwork grille instead of a plastic window. Only my father, who loved music and played records late into the night, was allowed to touch it.

My parents knew nothing about world politics, but they were proud of their daughter's newly acquired sophistication, so my sister Sally and I were summoned down from the nursery to listen in—not for our political education but to admire Anne's skills as a linguist. We sat in front of the big radiogram, listening to the Führer's crackly voice rising and falling through the static, while Anne stood beside it and translated, like a teacher in front of a class. I was only eight years old, but even I registered that the news was grim.

Every so often Hitler's ravings were punctuated by a great roar from the crowd: *"Sieg Heil! Sieg Heil! Sieg Heil!"*

Finally my mother spoke, "I don't like it much myself, but it's delicious the way Minnie does it," she said.

"Minnie?" said my father.

"Minnie, the cook. Who else?" my mother answered loftily. "She parboils it, then finishes it off with minced onion and butter."

"What in God's name are you talking about?" my father asked.

"Seakale," said my mother. "Of course, it's not in season at the moment."

Again, simply read this excerpt for your pleasure. Enter the scene of Alvarez's childhood in London back in 1938 when the Germans marched into Austria, when the elder sister came home from school in Switzerland upset by what was happening across the border and when his parents were seemingly oblivious to the Führer's ravings.

ELEMENT BY ELEMENT OF THE CHECKLIST
Now we'll take each element of the checklist and look at the excerpts of *Sula* and *Where Did It All Go Right?* to illustrate how to revise your own writing.

1. Leads and Endings
The first sentences in the two excerpts reveal the importance and power of the opening sentence. In *Sula,* "In that place, where they tore the nightshade and blackberry patches from their roots to make room for the Medallion City Golf Course, there was once a neighborhood" foretells the entire novel and evokes another world, one of nightshade and blackberry patches. In Alvarez's memoir, the date and the agitation of the sister coming back from her school in Switzerland call the reader to attention.

Look at your first sentence. Does it catch your attention? Would a reader want to continue? At the same time, does it announce or foretell the theme?

Look at your ending. Is it compatible with the beginning? In *Sula,* Morrison ends with a cry over the loss of Sula, "It was a fine cry but it had no bottom and it had no top, just circles and circles of sorrow." The words echo the opening. At the end of *Where Did It All Go Right?,* Alvarez returns to his father, thinking about what his father did with his life. He has come full circle, explaining that even as a writer, he did not want to be a spectator, but a player.

Is there resolution in your piece of writing? Is there new meaning? Is the protagonist moved? Make notes if there is work to be done here, and move to the second element.

✎ Exercise: Look at your lead and ending; make notes if necessary for a rewrite when you have more time. Five minutes.

2. Description

Look at the settings in the two excerpts. Wendell Berry says, "If you don't know where you are, you don't know who you are." Study the first sentence in *Sula* to learn how a sense of place pervades the work. Now look at how Alvarez describes the interior of the home. He is leading up to a description of London in 1938: the contrast, in order to surprise. Where is your story situated?

Look at the details of your descriptions. Stephen King writes that description begins in the writer's imagination but should finish in the reader's imagination. In *Sula* there are the blackberry patches, the singing and banjo playing, pool hall, the women at Irene's palace, the dark woman doing a bit of cakewalk, bare feet, saffron dust.

Now look at your work. Are the details vivid? Do they appeal to the senses? In *Where Did It All Go Right?* the description of the gramophone, a polished-walnut monster, draws the reader into the room. The Führer's crackly voice, the "Sieg Heil!" and then the details about his mother's culinary genius hold the reader in the scene.

✎ Exercise: Look at your description both of the setting and the characters. Rewrite. Again make notes for a further rewrite if necessary. Five minutes.

3. Dialogue

Is there dialogue? In *Sula,* there is no dialogue in the first few pages, but the writer's voice is so direct and intimate that the reader feels that Morrison is talking aloud. In *Where Did It All Go Right?,* the dialogue brings the scene to life and inserts humor into the foreboding atmosphere. If you have dialogue, does it add to the scene or is it static? Does it contribute to the characterization and the action? Is each voice that speaks unique? If there is no dialogue, would it enliven the piece to include it? Might you consider this?

✎ Exercise: Look at your use of dialogue. Rewrite if necessary. Five minutes.

4. Narrative Tug, Tension/Conflict

Are there opposites? In *Sula,* there is the Bottom (that is at the top) and there is the valley, there is the dark woman in the flowered dress and the valley man collecting rent. In

Where Did It All Go Right?, Alvarez creates tension by bringing alive the different characters, the earnest children, the bewildered father, and the scatterbrained mother. Humor contributes to the situation.

Look for the narrative tug created by causally related events. You have here only the opening page of each work, but you can sense that a story is starting to be told. Small crises are leading the reader forward. Is there this narrative tug in your piece? Think fairy tale, the "once upon a time" that triggers the story telling impulse in each of us. A story has a beginning, a middle, and an end. Does your piece? John Gardner writes in *The Art of Fiction* that by definition, "a story contains profluence, a requirement best satisfied by a sequence of causally related events that ends in a resolution."

What is the tense of your piece? If it is simple past, does it stay that way throughout? If you chose to write in the present, ask the same question. Respect the unity of tense. If you need to move further into the past or into the future, is the tense change well handled?

And finally, is the conflict important? The more important the conflict, the more important the story. The most important story, William Faulkner said, is "the heart in conflict with itself." Go back to the beginning of your piece. What is the desire, the need that sets the story in motion? Is it important? And who is preventing the protagonist from fulfilling this desire?

✎ Exercise: Look at the action, plot, and conflict. Rewrite and again make notes for more work if necessary. Five minutes.

5. Images, Similes, Metaphors, Symbols

You remember from Lesson Eight the importance of imagery in poetic prose—how you move from a simile (comparison of two images) to a metaphor (comparison without the words "like" or "as") to symbol (with added meaning). Which images are central to your piece? Toni Morrison speaks of the controlling image. She explains that in writing a story, once she knows that the patchwork quilt on the bed is orange and purple, she sees not only the room but the story. Read your piece and circle the images.

Look for similes and metaphors. In *Sula* the neighborhood stood in the hills and spread all the way to the river. "Stood" and "spread" are used as metaphors to give life to the place; it stood and it spread, like something that moves. The neighborhood once was alive. "A bit of black bottom": besides the alliteration (the repetition of "b") and the choice of the word "bottom," whatever the dance was, the reader imagines it, then follows the pain that rested under the eyelids, under the head rags, in the palm of the hand. Here, as elsewhere, metaphors make the pain real.

Where Did It All Go Right? employs the image of the gramophone, the monster as big as a modern washing machine, a simile that moves into metaphor, foreshadowing the monster in the next paragraph, the Führer.

In *The Art of Fiction,* Gardner speaks of symbolic association, writing that often in the writer's development of characters, atmosphere, and setting, there may appear unintentional repetitions of imagery. It is after the first draft, when the writer is reading over what he has written, that he may discover "these odd tics his unconscious has sent up to him." It may be a metaphor used directly, or a setting used metaphorically. This is the art of good writing. And you see it here, with the setting in *Sula* and with the gramophone as a monster in *Where Did It All Go Right?*.

✎ Exercise: Look at images: similes, metaphors, symbols. Rewrite and make notes for further revision if necessary. Ten minutes.

6. Genre and Shape, Whose Story, Point of View, Style, Rhythm, Voice

Genre: Genre refers broadly to the four genres: fiction, nonfiction, drama, and poetry, whereas subgenres refer to the many different forms: journal entry, essay, commentary, tale, flash fiction, prose poem, dialogue, monologue, profile, parody, satire, song lyrics, and still more. Think about your piece of writing. First, have you written it as fiction or nonfiction? Why? If it is imagined, it is clearly fiction. If it is from your life, you still have a choice. Which works better for this piece? Is the subgenre (fairy tale, flash fiction, dialogue, prose poem, journal entry, etc.) well chosen? Does it correspond to the shape of your story?

Whose story is it? Sometimes the writer is not sure. If you think of Flannery O'Connor's story "Everything That Rises Must Converge," Julian escorts his mother to the Y for her reducing class. They argue all the while about the mother's new hat, about the passengers on the bus. The tension rises between Julian's disgust with his mother's racial prejudices, and the mother's long-lasting reproach to her son. Finally the mother is struck by an angry passenger and falls to the sidewalk with a stroke. Julian runs into the distance yelling for help. Whose story is it? So much of the action is around the mother. But it is Julian's story. He is the moved character. Only when he sees his mother helpless does he realize his blame. Think about the question: whose story is it?

Point of view: From what perspective is your piece written? Here is a very brief summary (for more detail return to Lesson Four, Short Story and the Short-Short). If your piece is a personal essay, it will be written in first person, the author being the narrator. If it is fiction, you have the choice of first person (using "I"), second person (using "you"—extremely rare, yet note one example, "Little Red Returns" in Lesson Seven, Tales), third person (using "he" or "she," and with a further choice—subjective or objective), omniscient (everyone's point of view), or multiple (skipping around among a few characters). Your choice depends in a large part upon the distance you wish to give between the reader and the narrator, the person who has the point of view. Look at your story and consider if the point of view is correct. Would it be better told in another point of view?

Style: Is your style of writing adapted to your story? Is it pleasing, is it consistent? Style runs from objective to subjective, from the discursive style of the essayist to the anecdotal or ironic style of the storyteller to the lyrical style of the poet. Literary styles come and go; what is most important is to remember that the style reflects the writer. In *The Elements of Style,* William Strunk, Jr. writes that style takes its final shape more from the attitudes of the mind than the principles of composition. And in *The Art of Fiction,* Gardner points out that most styles are traditional and many writers master one of them. Then slowly his personality modifies it, making it sound different from another writer's style. Some writers change their style according to the story and the genre. Some writers wish to be innovative, but this may pull too much attention to the style itself. Overall, it is best to avoid style's excesses. Now consider the style of your piece of writing. Does it fit you, the writer? Does it fit the story? Is it consistent?

Rhythm: Read your piece aloud. Listen to its rhythm. If your voice catches, go back and check the words and syllables. In Lesson Eight, Poetic Prose, we worked with meter in relation to our prose, looking at where the accents fall in a sentence. We worked with sounds: with words that sound like what they are describing (onomatopoeia), with the repetition of consonants (alliteration) and vowels (assonance), and with the repetition of words and phrases. Look again at your work. Listen to it. Have you crafted the words and sentences carefully for their sounds?

Voice: Voice is different from style. It is the vehicle by which a writer expresses his vitality, his morality, his world vision. Philip Roth tells us in *The Ghost Writer* that voice begins at the back of the knees and reaches way above the head. The writer speaks from the center of his being. The writer does not find his voice, but the voice finds the writer. Julia Cameron writes in *The Right to Write* that each of us has a voice, and that rather than working to develop it we need rather to uncover it. Hence the reason for her morning pages, first proposed in *The Artist's Way,* then developed in her following books. Cameron urges the reader to write regularly every morning from the gut. Is your voice strong? The voice in a story is its body language. Does your voice have muscle? Does your piece of writing stand on its own? Is it full-bodied?

✎ Exercise: Look at genre, whose story is it, point of view, style, voice. Rewrite if necessary. Make notes for further rewriting. Ten minutes.

7. Theme and Meaning

What is the theme (the subject) of your piece of writing? Given your choice of subject, are your ideas clear? Here every writer has to pay attention to clutter. Writing is hard work, good work. It centers us. It clarifies our thinking. This lets us get rid of clutter: unnecessary prepositions, adjectives, and adverbs. William Zinsser in *On Writing Well* says that his own first drafts can be cut by 50 percent. They are swollen with words that do not do new work. Look for clutter in your piece and prune it ruthlessly.

What is the meaning of the piece? Is it worth the story? Does it resonate? It should not be too evident, but neither should it be hidden. Give it to your reader as a gift that the reader must unwrap herself. She will be all the more grateful.

✎ Exercise: Consider your theme, delete the clutter, and make the meaning resonant. Rewrite if necessary. Ten minutes.

8. Editing (after the work has been revised)

When you have rewritten your piece, when you feel that you have gone as far as you can go for the moment, then think about the editing. Remember Hemingway writing the ending of *Farewell to Arms* thirty-nine times. And of course, when and while you are editing, you can still rewrite!

My suggestions for editing are short and quick:

— Title: Does it fit? Does it call for the reader's attention? You have worked with titles throughout this book; you know their importance. Be tough with yourself. Look at your title. Does it work?

— Length: Look at the length of your piece, at the length of each paragraph, at the length of each sentence. There should be variation. The reader should be able to catch his breath.

— Verbs: Get rid of all passive verbs, including verbs of being. Look at the difference between "The table looked like it was sagging." And "The table sagged." Use active verbs.

— Unnecessary words: Delete adverbs, extra adjectives, clichés, and pet words (unless they are useful in dialogue to characterize someone). Mark Twain is said to have commented, "Adverbs, don't."

— Visual effect: Look at how the piece will appear, placement of paragraphs, space, and centering.

— Proofread: Again, read for consistency (tense of verbs, point of view), punctuation, and spelling.

✎ Exercise: Edit your piece. Do this fairly quickly for now. You will be able to go back and do more later. Ten minutes.

Now is the time to share your work with a group, or with a friend, for critiquing. Welcome the suggestions that other writers make as they read or listen to your words. Do not try to defend your work; instead, appreciate the feedback.

The last step in this lesson is finding a home for your piece. When you finally feel ready to send it out into the world, see it as a gift that will come back to you. I remember well the first letter I received from a reader. It was in response to a personal essay about my grandfather's schoolhouse in the Philippines, published in the *Christian Science Monitor*. A few months afterward, I received a letter from a woman in Seattle. She had seen the essay, checked the dates, and read it to her mother, who was blind and living in a home for the elderly. Her mother listened, started paying close attention, smiled, then wept. She had been one of the teachers sent a generation later to take over from my grandfather. This can happen to you. The stories are yours. Share them. Together our voices will resonate and reach around the world.

The end of this lesson includes, along with the checklist for rewriting, a page with suggestions for marketing and getting published. It is a sheet that I share in my workshops, which I constantly update. I share it with you, asking you now to update it and share it as well.

✎ The exercises fit into a two-hour lesson. The first four are short, the next four are long. If you wish to work on rewriting over the month, I would suggest that you do the four short ones the first week. This would let you do the first of the longer exercises, working with the images, the second week, then the next longer exercise (genre, whose story, point of view, style, rhythm, voice) the third week, and the following exercise (theme and meaning) the fourth week. Then put the piece aside for awhile before editing. A rewritten work needs also to gestate!

CHECKLIST FOR REWRITING
(Revising)

1. Leads and Endings

    —Does first paragraph (first line) capture the reader's attention?

    —Is the piece well framed? Does it begin too early, too late? End too early, too late?

    —Are lead and ending compatible? Is there foreshadowing?

    —Is there a feeling of resolution? Does the protagonist change? Is there new meaning?

    —Is it closed or open-ended? Wrapped up but still alive?

2. Description (characterization and setting)

    —Does each setting contribute to story?

    —Show! Is description vivid, specific? Does it touch the senses?

    —Are characters alive?

3 Dialogue

    —Does the dialogue advance the characterization and story?

    —Does it contribute to the tone?

    —Is each character's voice dialogue unique?

4. 4. Narrative Tug, Tension/Conflict

    —Is there tension through opposites in settings, characters, dialogue?

—Is there a narrative tug, "profluence" (John Gardner)?

—Is the struggle worth the story?

5. Images, Similes, Metaphors, Symbols

　　—Are there central (controlling) images?

　　—Are there comparisons (similes/metaphors)?

　　—Are there deeper associations and substitutions (symbols)?

6. Genre and Shape, Whose Story, Point of View, Style, Rhythm, Voice

　　—Does the shape fit the story? Is the genre/subgenre right for both the story and author?

　　—Whose story is it?

　　—In what point of view?

　　—Is the style appropriate to the subject (poetic, didactic, humorous)?

　　—Is the rhythm consistent (scanning for meter, word sounds, repetition)?

　　—Is author's voice full-bodied and consistent?

7. Theme and Meaning

　　—What is the subject (theme)?

　　—Is there clutter? Are the writer's ideas clear?

　　—Is there a moment of new awareness (Joyce's "epiphany")?

　　—Why is the story important?

8. Editing

    —Title (Does it fit? Does it grab attention?)

    —Length (too short/too long?)

    —Sentence and paragraphs (varied/monotonous?)

    —Verbs (active/passive? avoid verbs of being)

    —Unnecessary words (adverbs, adjectives, clichés, complicated words, pet words, dialogue tags)

    —Visual effect (placement of paragraphs, white space, dialogue)

SUGGESTIONS FOR MARKETING-PUBLISHING

1. Tools

—Web: google, www.writersmarket.com, www.writermag.com (2,500 markets updated weekly), www.thunderburst.co.uk (Dee Rimbaud, Independent Press Guide), www.literary-marketplace.com.

—Magazines: Poets & Writers, Writer's Digest, The Writer, Writers' News, Writers' Forum, Mylexia

—Books: Writer's Market (Writer's Digest, 6,500 listings), Writer's Handbook (The Writer, 3000 listings), Writers' and Artist's Yearbook (A&C Black, London), International Directory of Little Magazines and Small Presses (Dustbooks), Into Print (Poets & Writers)

—Networks: workshops, conferences, associations, Associated Writers and Writing Programs (www.awpwriter.org); Authors' Guild (www.authorsguild.org), International Women's Writing Guild (www.iwwg.org); Society of Children's Books Writers & Illustrators (www.scbwi.org)

2. Steps

—Know the field (study the markets)

—Target ideas, target markets (read several issues of publications and submission guidelines)

—Query and cover letters (examples in Writers' Market, specialized books, websites)

—Bio: credentials (publication credits, teaching experience, writing degrees, associations), platform. (your place in the world, your visibility, your network). If you have no credentials: refer briefly to why you wrote the article/book

—Book proposal and synopsis (again, read examples)

—Record submissions (use a double system: by title and by date)

—Handling rejections: be patient and continue to write

3. Publishing

—Finding an agent: Association of Authors' Representatives (www.aar-online.org), IWWG (list at www.iwwg.org), www.writers.net/forum; www.anotherealm.com/prededitors, acknowledgements in books you like

—Without an agent: network; consider other ways of publishing

—Resources: www.editorsandpredators (listings of agents and publishers)

—Royalty publishers (traditional, trade) versus subsidy publishers (sharing costs) versus vanity publishers (authors pay enormous sums, sometimes then have to buy back their own copies)

—Self-publishing (publishing on your own), print-on-demand (publishing with a printer who formats your book, prints copies, sells them to you and online): www.Iuniverse.com, www.Xlibris.com, www.authorhouse.com (sold 1 million volumes in 2003)

—Short-run book publishing (publishing with a printer a limited number of copies): www.lulu.com

—Electronic publishing: Journal of Electronic Publishing www.press.umich.edu/jep; NY Times' "Digital Publishing Is Scrambling the Industry's Rules," June 5 2006

—Blog to book: "Sometimes it pays to blog" (The Writer, February 2007) The Wandering Scribe, Anya Peters; How Would a Patriot Act? Glenn Greenwald, Julie and Julia, Julie Powell

—Chapbooks: wikipedia (listing different collections of chap books), "The Origin and Evolution of Chapbooks," Poets and Writers, November/December '98

4. How to get from where you are to where you wish to be
—Read (fiction, nonfiction, poetry, and professional magazines)
—Be open to the world
—Start in small markets
—Explore workshops, conferences, MFA programs (lists in Poets & Writers)
—Remain true to your feelings; write every day; keep submitting

Writing the Way Home

You have written your way through twelve lessons. Starting with journal entries, you moved to essays (personal, opinion, and travel) and to short stories. On the second stretch, you tapped deeper into your creative voice, working with dreams, then imagining dialogues, writing fairy tales, and crafting poetic prose. Alchemy took you still deeper on the third stretch, and you looked at mosaics, memoirs, and rewriting—re-visioning your words.

This last month portrays writing—in whatever genre—as the way home. In *The Writing Life* Annie Dillard says, "Words lead to other words and down the garden path." Down the garden path and home. You enter into the labyrinth of being and find your true home in the center. The world today is fragmented—a vision of one peaceful world is more elusive than ever. There is a longing for community, for a sense of belonging. A longing for home. Your words will address this longing, bringing light into your own life and the world around you.

LONGING FOR HOME

In our contemporary world, many of us live our lives moving on and scattering, rather than connecting and gathering. The ravages of 9/11, the Indian Ocean tsunami of 2004, Hurricane Katrina, the wars and violence in the Middle East, the genocide and hunger in Africa all make us feel insecure. How do you find a place to rest, a homeland? I suggest calling upon Hestia, the Greek goddess of the hearth, and through your writing, kindling her flame in the center of your home.

Hestia was one of the most important of the Greek goddesses, yet today she is virtually unknown. She was the sister of Zeus, who gave her the keys to Mount Olympus where she faithfully tended the sacred fire. In ancient Greece there was a hearth in the center of every home where the day began and ended with a prayer to Hestia. Each newborn child was carried around her hearth before being received into the family. Likewise every city had a public hearth where the fire was never allowed to go out for it represented the spiritual life of the city. When a new colony was to be founded, coals and embers were carried from the hearth of the mother city. In Rome Hestia, as Vesta, had her temple in the Forum. Inside the round temple burned the eternal fire, the symbolic hearth of Rome and all Romans. Where is this flame today?

Hestia is the archetype of centeredness, of wholeness; her symbol is the circle. When you celebrate Hestia, you celebrate your own wholeness and the wholeness of the universe. In your writing, early in the morning when you journal, or during the day when you work on a story or an essay or on longer works of fiction or nonfiction, you are tending your own hearth and carrying embers to the world hearth. Your writing moves from the personal to the universal.

You may call upon Hestia as the bards of ancient times did, as Homer did.

HOMERIC HYMN TO HESTIA

Hestia, you who tend the holy house of the lord Apollo, with soft oil dripping from your locks, come now into this house, come, having one mind with Zeus, draw near and [bestow] grace upon my song.

May Hestia come into your home and bestow grace upon your writing.

FINDING IMAGES THAT LEAD HOMEWARD

To celebrate Hestia, you need to find the images in your life that center you, images that gather together rather than scatter apart. The poet within you knows that some images take you to the core—the matrix that May Sarton wrote about in *Journal of a Solitude*—where your creativity is embedded. I have shown how I use such images: the little cinquefoil that was so light in my hand that it took me to my father and his ashes; the crooked pear tree in my front yard that led me closer to my mother-in-law, stricken with Alzheimers' disease.

By finding these images and following them home through writing—from journaling to essays to prose poems—you approach Hestia's hearth and connect to the core of your creativity. To help uncover these images, return once again to the words of Rainer Maria Rilke in his *Letters to a Young Poet:* "There is only one thing you should do. Go into yourself." And as you did in earlier chapters, look for images—in your dreams, memories, and surroundings—that resonate and lead you homeward to your center.

DREAMS

Remembering that dreams open the door to our deeper selves, let's go within and look at the images in our dreams. I included an introduction to dreams in Lesson Five. In this lesson, you will look for centering images. Here is a dream from Terry Tempest William's book *Leap,* a book that leads the readers in and out of Bosch's "Garden of Delights."

FROM THE CHAPTER "EARTHLY DELIGHTS"

I dreamed this center panel long before I saw it. I was walking through the Hayden Valley of Yellowstone. It was autumn and the grasses along the river had turned to gold. Steam was rising from pink and blue furnaces. The stench of sulphur was strong. Mud pots hidden in the forests were bubbling. There were people everywhere, human beings engaged in Earthplay.

Everyone, everything was in motion.

Yellow Grizzlies. Blue Bison. Red Ravens. Elk wearing bridles of silver led by Coyotes in pink capes at dawn . . . I awoke in a sweat. That is all I remembered until I stood before the triptych in the Prado and realized El Bosco had painted my dream.

Williams remembers the dream and moves with delight from the yellow grizzlies and coyotes in pink capes to the triptych that she has discovered in the Prado museum in Madrid. Here, men and women and children are chanting and offering her a chance to enjoy the Garden of Delights, the middle panel that had been closed to her eyes throughout her childhood: images from her dream leading to her real home.

Here is how novelist Isabel Allende follows the images of her dreams. In Writers Dreaming, Allende explains how dreams are like a storage room where "in that dreamy state, you can reach in the darkness and find something like a treasure." With her first novel, *House of Spirits,* she had written the last pages over and over but could not get them right. Then she woke one night with a dream of her grandfather, lying on his bed, dressed entirely in black on his black bed and she was sitting on a black chair, dressed also in black and telling him she had written a book. She realized that her dream image showed the way to end her novel with the death of the grandfather, and the grand-daughter sitting at his side, telling his story.

Now it's your turn. Find a dream that calls to you, that speaks to you, perhaps, of your childhood. First, go within and close your eyes. What dream comes to you? A recent dream or one from long ago? Take your time. Let the dream surface on its own.

✎ Exercise: Free-write the dream. Five minutes.

Before we move to memories, read the dream that you have just written. Circle any image that resonates. Look for those that hint of home. If there is not an image that vibrates, close your eyes again. What image comes to you? Perhaps one from your child-hood. Jot it down.

✎ Exercise: Circle an image in your dream. A few minutes.

MEMORIES

Now look at your memories, those that lead you homeward.
Here is a passage from an essay by Wallis Wilde-Menozzi,
included in *The Best Spiritual Writing 2002,* where she is
remembering her visit to the Church of the Holy Trinity at the
Monastery of St. Sergiyev—once known as Zagorsk—outside
Moscow.

FROM THE ESSAY "THE ONENESS OF MUSIC"

Imagine candles, thin, papery, fine, rising and clinging on
chandeliers, candles burning like the hives of God, flames so
abundant and busy that they hiss and send up bursts of
unmeasurable light in a damp heavy dark; then feel monks
with strong faces and ardent voices and hear other human
voices sunk into a darkness so thick and contrasting that the
eyes coming in from outside can barely make out a way in
those mystifying contrasts of blaze and dark. Then imagine
voices singing the liturgy of centuries. Imagine ancient
plainchants that reach back into time, nearly eternal non-
Western time, and the embrace of improvising voices that
harmonize using polyphonic lines to reveal another melody.
The voices swerving and winding their way through the
darkness surrounded me and swept me away.

The candles burn and hiss like the hives of God. Wilde-Menozzi
not only hears the ardent voices of the monks, she feels them.
The contrasts of blaze and dark mystify. The ancient plainchants
reach back into another time as the embrace of harmonizing

voices reveals a deeper melody. A memory leading the author to experience the oneness of her world, our world.

Here is a childhood memory from Carlos Eire's memoir *Waiting for Snow in Havana*. In 1962, Eire was one of the 14,000 children airlifted out of Cuba, exiled from family and country by the revolution. His memory of the day that Batista flew out of Cuba opens his memoir.

From Chapter One *"Uno"*

The world changed while I slept, and much to my surprise, no one had consulted me. That's how it would always be from that day forward . . .

I was barely eight years old and I had spent hours dreaming of childish things, as children do . . .

The tropical sun knifed through the gaps in the wooden shutters, as always, extending in narrow shafts of light above my bed, revealing entire galaxies of swirling dust specks. I stared at the dust, as always, rapt. I don't remember getting out of bed. But I do remember walking into my parents' bedroom. Their shutters were open and the room was flooded with light. As always my father was putting on his trousers over his shoes . . .

As he slid his baggy trousers over his brown wingtip shoes, Louis XVI [his father's prior incarnation] broke the news to me: "Batista is gone. He flew out of Havana early this morning. It looks like the rebels have won."

"You lie," I said.

"No, I swear it's true," he replied.

Eire remembers that morning as the morning his childhood was finished. Up until then, there were his home, his childish dreams, his parents' bedroom flooded with early morning light, his father's baggy trousers. After that morning, this world disappeared. It slipped into his memory, waiting to be revived in writing.

Just as you did with a dream, now find a memory that resonates. It can be of your childhood, or of a more recent time, perhaps traveling somewhere. First go within and close your eyes. What memory comes to you? A memory that centers you, gathers you together. Try to empty your mind and let the memory find you.

✎ Exercise: Free-write the memory. Five minutes.

Now read the memory. Again, circle images that resonate. Look for centering images, ones that lead homeward. And if there is not an image that catches your attention, close your eyes and see what image comes to you. Write it down very briefly.

✎ Exercise: Circle an image in your memory. A few minutes.

SURROUNDINGS

Finally, look for images in your surroundings. Go for a walk. Look around you, inside your home, outside your home. What images call your attention? Here is another page from *An Interrupted Life,* the journals of Ettie Hillesum during the last two years of her life. She is writing on her way to Westerbork, the transit camp for the Jews in Holland before they were packed into the freight wagons off to Poland, to Auschwitz.

FROM THE ENTRY, SUNDAY NIGHT [SEPTEMBER 20, 1942]
Jopie [a close friend] on the heath sitting under the great,
big starry sky, talking about nostalgia. I have no nostalgia
left, I feel at home. I have learned so much about it here. We
are "at home." Under the sky. In every place on earth, if only
we carry everything within us.
. . . We must be our own country.

The image is of the sky, one same sky for all of us, for her friend
Jopie, for herself, for both of them, above the barbed wire at
Westerbork. In her writing, Ettie Hillesum found her home
within herself. She is her own country.

And now here is an example from inside the home, inside a
room. Artist and poet Karen McDermott wrote a poem (*Offshoots, Writing from Geneva,* VII) about three pears in a shallow
earthen bowl. The image took the writer to family, bound by the
secret of seed.

"THREE PEARS"
  Three pears
  bump up
  like hills receding
  on the light of late afternoon.

  Only a thin skin
  green mottled brown
  holds back the swelling
  unsuspected marvel of moisture.
  The slightest tremor sets them
  rolling, jostling one another

just three after all
they settle again

precarious, poised
each holding the other
momentarily in place, pears
bound by chance, by the curled lip

of an earthen bowl, bound
like family
by the secret of seed
and hidden heart.

An image of pears held momentarily in place by the curled lip of a bowl leads the poet inward to hidden hearts.

Now find an image from your surroundings that speaks of where you live. In your imagination, go for a walk inside your house. What image calls to you? What image welcomes you every day, centering you? Then go for a walk outside, into your front yard, your backyard, or along a favorite path. Is there an image that often catches your attention? Choose one image, let it choose you. Write about it. What is its story?

✎ Exercise: Write about an image from your surroundings, from inside your home or outside. Five minutes.

FOLLOWING THE IMAGE HOME

It is time to follow one of the images that you have circled, letting it lead you to Hestia's hearth within, to a deeper sense of self. First go back to the images you circled in your dream, in your memory, and the image of your surroundings. Choose just one of these. Which one hints of home? This will be the image that you will work with during the rest of this lesson.

DRAWING A LABYRINTH

The labyrinth is an ancient symbol relating to wholeness. The oldest one dates back over four thousand years, the Cretan Labyrinth associated with the myth of Theseus and the Minotaur. Perhaps the best-known one was the Chartres Labyrinth, laid in the floor of Chartres Cathedral in France around 1220. It was meant to be walked as a pilgrimage, a questing journey to replace the pilgrimage to Jerusalem that was too far away for most pilgrims. Labyrinths have long been used as spiritual exercises in different religious traditions. The one feature they all share is that they have one path winding to the center and the same path winding back out. Labyrinths are often confused with mazes. A maze has twists and turns and blind alleys. A labyrinth has only one path. In this exercise you will draw a labyrinth, following your image from the entrance to the center, where Hestia will be waiting for you.

The renewed interest in labyrinths today corresponds to our growing search for meaning, for community, for belonging in our contemporary lives. When we walk a labyrinth, there are three stages:

—releasing, a letting go of thoughts and distractions as we walk to the center
—receiving, a centering as we reach the center and stay as long as we wish
—returning, a leaving along the same path with a renewed spirit

Seen in this way, the labyrinth is a metaphor for the journey to the center of the self and back out into the world with a broadened understanding of who we are. Drawing labyrinths— or mandalas and meanders—are ways of visualizing our images. They are ways of doing active imagination that Jung defined as the active engaging of our images until they connect the visible with the invisible. The images then become uniting symbols, bringing together the known and the unknown.

Here are two simple labyrinths I drew at different times. The one on the left side is among the first that I drew. I was concerned about the technique. I almost forgot to follow an image. It is a very careful labyrinth. The one to the right I drew more recently. I was looking out the window near my desk at the red and pink begonia blossoms in the flower boxes on either side of my small back yard. The blossoms led me to the center of my labyrinth. I was more relaxed. If you let your hand draw the labyrinth, you will see the difference.

Following to the Center

Following Begonia Blossoms

It is your turn. For this workshop, I ask you to place Hestia's hearth in the center of your labyrinth. Now take a blank sheet of paper and draw the large outer circle, with the entrance most easily at the bottom of your circle. Place a dot in the center, there where Hestia is waiting for you. Imagine your image at the entrance. Let the image lead your hand as you draw a path, circling back and forth, not necessarily in full circles, almost closing your eyes, following your image as it makes its way to the center. Do not worry about drawing the two sides of the path; just the single line will be the path. Draw slowly, following the image homeward.

✎ Exercise: Draw a labyrinth. Ten minutes. Once you have drawn your labyrinth, look at it and give it a title.

Now enter your labyrinth with your index finger. Remember to let your image lead you. As your finger moves along the path, let go of distractions and of what diffuses your attention. When you arrive in the center, let yourself rest for a moment, close to Hestia's hearth. Then slowly return back to the world outside. Imagine that you are carrying some of the embers out into the world around you, just as the ancient Greeks did when they left their cities to found new colonies.

✎ Exercise: Follow your labyrinth with your index finger. A few minutes.

DIALOGUING WITH THE IMAGE

This second exercise involves writing a dialogue. Listen to your image. Ask it why it came to you today. What does it want to say to you? Be quiet. Try not to think out the answers, nor the questions that follow. Simply write a dialogue. For example, I ask the begonia blossoms why they came to me. "To take you to both sides," they reply. "Why?" "For balance." Now start the dialogue with yourself, asking the image why it came to you. Then let the image answer. And follow along, writing down whatever the two of you are saying to one another. You and your image. Your image and you. Let yourself be surprised.

✎ Exercise: Write a dialogue. Ten minutes.

GIVING THE IMAGE ROOTS

As in all exercises of active imagination, it is important to note what happened in writing. Very often, when you wake up from a dream you feel enriched, amazingly alive. However, if you do not write it down, the dream disappears back into your unconscious. In the same way, although not as obvious, when you grow aware of a new dimension in your life, if you do not write it down, you later belittle it. You are apt to say to yourself, "Oh, that was nothing—a passing intuition." But it is precisely these passing intuitions that let you live on a deeper level, that let you write on a deeper level, and that finally give you a deeper sense of belonging to this world of yours. These are the flashes of inspiration that come to you when you are centered. They are the flames of Hestia that you have kindled and that you now take back out into the world.

Here is what Dag Hammarskjöld, the United Nations General Secretary, wrote in his journal *Markings,* about discovering this center of our being.

From *Markings*, 1959, 8.4.59

In the point of rest at the center of our being, we encounter a world where all things are at rest in the same way. Then a tree becomes a mystery, a cloud a revelation, each man a cosmos of whose riches we can only catch glimpses. The life of simplicity is simple, but it opens to us a book in which we never get beyond the first syllable.

Whenever you enter the center of your being, be it just for a brief moment, you need to write it down. This way you track your journey through life. Markings.

It is your turn to write about your image. How you followed it, how it led you to the center of the labyrinth, where you rested with it close to Hestia's fire. Write in whatever form comes to you—a journal entry, a personal essay, a short story, a dialogue, or a prose poem. Take your time to do this. Perhaps describe the image in the first paragraph. Next, describe where it took you. What did you discover? What embers from your hearth—your heart—can you share with the reader?

✎ Exercise: Write a journal entry, personal essay, short story, or prose poem about your image. Fifteen minutes. Remember the importance of naming and give it a title.

Look at this last piece of writing as a flame from Hestia's hearth that you found in writing your way home. Think of Ettie Hillesum there in the transit barracks of Westerbork, with the world around her blown to pieces, how she wrote her way home. How even behind the barbed wire fences, she found her home within herself. One home under the one same sky, "the great big starry sky."

There is an ancient metaphor for this starry sky, the Hindu image of Indra's net. Over the palace of the God Indra, as written in the *Vedas* back in 1500 BCE, there hung a vast network of precious jewels with a jewel at each intersection of threads. The jewels were so arranged that each reflected all the other jewels of the net. The net was infinite in dimension, just as the jewels were infinite in number. A change in one jewel made for a change, however slight, in all the other jewels.

Indra's net is a contemporary metaphor for the holographic nature of our universe, where every point is interconnected to all other points. What one of us does affects all the others. It is a metaphor that expresses our one same sky, our one same home-land. Here is the world of Hestia, the world of wholeness where each one of us keeps our flame alive, lighting the hearths in our homes and in our cities.

Once you have embarked on the journey of writing, you are writing your way home. A lightbearer in the world.

✎ In this last lesson there are three short exercises (writing a dream, a memory, and something in your surroundings) and three longer exercises (drawing a labyrinth, writing a dialogue, and writing the story of your journey home). As in each lesson, the exercises can be followed one after the other, with the suggested time limits, or they can be spread out over the month. If you choose this way, the first three could be done the first week, then each of the longer exercises each following week.

Bibliographies and Page References by Lessons

There are many excellent resources for writers available in print and online. The lists below represent only a small portion. You will discover your own favorites as you continue along the path of your writing life.

Introduction

Cameron, Julia, *The Right to Write* (New York: Jeremy Tarcher/Putnam, 1999), xvii.

Dillard, Annie, *The Writing Life* (New York: Harper & Row, 1989), 11.

Jung, Carl G., *Memories, Dreams, Reflections* (London: Fontana Paperbacks, 1969), 107.

King, Stephen, *On Writing* (New York: Scribner, 2000), 269.

Lesson One: Journal Writing

Cameron, Julia, *The Artist's Way* (New York: Tarcher/Putnam, 1992).

Elbow, Peter, *Writing with Power* (Oxford: Oxford University Press, 1981).

Goldberg, Natalie, *Writing Down the Bones* (Boston: Shambhala, 1986).

Heilbrun, Carolyn, *Writing a Woman's Life* (New York: Ballantine, 1988).

Hillesum, Ettie, *An Interrupted Life* (New York: Henry Holt, 1986), 94–96.

Holzer, Burghild Nina, *A Walk Between Heaven and Earth* (New York: Bell Tower, 1994), 14.

Jung, Carl G., *Memories, Dreams, Reflections,* 223.

Kelly, Susan, "With George Plimpton," *Country and Abroad,* June 1998, 6.

Sarton, May, *Journal of a Solitude* (New York: Norton, 1973), 11–12.

Schiwy, Marlene, *A Voice of Her Own* (New York: Simon & Schuster, 1996).

Ueland, Brenda, *If You Want to Write* (St. Paul, MN: Graywolf, 1987), 140.

Woodman, Marion, *Bone: Dying to Life* (New York: Viking, 2000), xi.

LESSON TWO: PERSONAL ESSAYS

Atwan, Robert, ed., *The Best American Essays 2001* (Boston: Houghton Mifflin, 2001).

Capote, Truman, *In Cold Blood* (New York: Vintage International, 1991).

Clay, George, "When Everything Begins" in *Fourth Genre* (East Lansing, MI: Michigan State University Press, Spring 2001), 85.

Dillard, Annie, Introduction, *Best American Essays* 1988 (Boston: Houghton Mifflin, 1988)

Goldberg, Natalie, *Writing Down the Bones.*

Gutkind, Lee, *The Art of Creative Nonfiction* (New York: Wiley, 1997).

Hirsch, Kathleen, "The Return of the Essay" (profile of Robert Atwan), *Poets & Writers Magazine,* November/December 1995.

King, Stephen, *On Writing.*

Lopate, Phillip, *The Art of the Personal Essay: An Anthology from the Classical Era to the Present* (New York: Doubleday, 1994).

Lott, Bret, "Genesis," *Creative Nonfiction #27* (Pittsburgh: *Creative Nonfiction,* 2005), 30–31.

———, "Toward a Definition of Creative Nonfiction," *Fourth Genre,* Spring 2000, 195.

Norris, Kathleen, *Dakota: A Spiritual Geography* (Boston: Houghton Mifflin, 1993).

Rilke, Rainer Maria, *Letters to a Young Poet* (New York: Norton, 1962), 29.

Root, Robert L., Jr. and Michael Steinberg, *The Fourth Genre,* second ed. (New York: Longman, 2001).

Steinberg, Michael, ed., *Fourth Genre,* Spring 2000.

Tiberghien, Susan, "In a Grocery Far from Home," *International Herald Tribune,* October 18, 1992.

LESSON THREE: OPINION AND TRAVEL ESSAYS

Guidelines for writers: *New York Times* (www.nytimes.com); *Christian Science Monitor* (www.csmonitor.com); National Academy Op-Ed Service (www.nationalacademies.org); *Islands* (www.islands.com); *Condé Nast Traveler* (www. cntraveler.com); *Travelers' Tales* (www.travelerstales.com)

Hiestand, Emily, "Renewing the Sun" in McCauley, Lucy, Amy C. Carlson, and Jennifer Leo, eds., *A Woman's Path: Women's Best Spiritual Travel Writing* (Berkeley, CA: Travelers' Tales, 2000), 40–41.

Kingsolver, Barbara, *Small Wonder* (London: Faber & Faber, 2002), 180–181.

Lemack, Carie, "9/11 means heroism—and division," *International Herald Tribune,* September 10–11, 2005.

Stevens, Sidney, "When Times Were Tough" ("My Turn" essay), *Newsweek,* July 28, 2003.

Wilson, Jason, series editor, *Best American Travel Writing* (Boston: Houghton Mifflin, 2006).

Zinsser, William, *On Writing Well,* fourth edition (New York: Harper Perennial, 1990).

LESSON FOUR: SHORT STORIES AND THE SHORT-SHORT

Gardner, Janet E., "Gifts," *Vestal Review,* 2005, www.vestal review.net/Gifts.htm

Gardner, John, *The Art of Fiction* (New York: Vintage, 1984), 31.

Guthrie, A.B., *A Field Guide to Writing Fiction* (New York: HarperCollins, 1991).

Hills, Rush, *Writing in General and the Short Story in Particular* (Boston: Houghton Mifflin, 1987).

Joyce, James, "The Dead," *Dubliners* (London: Penguin Modern Classics, 2000), 168.

Lamott, Anne, *Bird by Bird* (New York: Doubleday, 1995).

O'Connor, Flannery, *Mystery and Manners* (New York: Farrar, Straus and

Giroux, 1984).

Paley, Grace, "Wants" in Howe, Irving and Ilana Wiener Howe, eds., *Short Shorts* (London: Bantam, 1983), 171–73.

Passaro, Vince, "Unlikely Stories," *Harper's,* August 1999.

Rainer, Tristine, *Your Life as Story* (New York: Tarcher/Putnam, 1998).

Scarfe, Eunice, "When My Mourning Comes," © Eunice Scarfe, Banff, Alberta, 2002.

Shapard, Robert & James Thomas, eds., *Sudden Fiction International: 60 Short-Short Stories* (New York: Norton, 1989).

———, *Sudden Fiction Continued: 60 New Short-Short Stories* (New York: Norton, 1996).

———, *New Sudden Fiction* (New York: Norton, 2007).

Thomas, James, Denise Thomas, and Tom Hazuka, eds., *Flash Fiction, 72 Very Short Stories* (New York: Norton, 1992).

Wilson, Kevin, "Carried Away," *Quick Fiction,* Issue Four (Jamaica Plain, MA), 2003, 18–19.

LESSON FIVE: DREAMS AND WRITING

Angelou, Maya in Epel, Naomi, ed., *Writers Dreaming* (New York: Vintage, 1994), 30.

Bosnak, Robert, *A Little Course in Dreams* (Boston: Shambhala, 1988.)

Epel, Naomi, ed., *Writers Dreaming.*

Illuminations of Hildegard of Bingen, commentary by Matthew Fox (Santa Fe: Bear & Co., 1985).

Jung, C G., *Civilization in Transition,* second ed. (Princeton:

Princeton University Press, 1970).

———, *Memories, Dreams, Reflections.*

Ondaatje, Michael, *Running in the Family* (London: Picador, 1984), 21.

Price, Reynolds in Epel, Naomi, ed., *Writers Dreaming,* 202.

Styron, William in Epel, ed., *Writers Dreaming,* 272.

Tiberghien, Susan, *Looking for Gold* (Einsiedeln, Switzerland: Daimon Books,

1997).

Udall, Brady, "The Wig," *Story Magazine,* Cincinnati: F&W Publications, 1994.

Ueland, Brenda, *If You Want to Write.*

Van de Castle, Robert, *Our Dreaming Mind* (New York, Ballantine, 1994).

Vivian, Robert, "Light Calling to Other Light," *Fourth Genre,* Spring 2000, 60-61.

Walker, Alice, *Living by the Word* (New York: Harcourt, 1988).

LESSON SIX: DIALOGUE

Chevalier, Tracey, *Girl with a Pearl Earring* (London: HarperCollins, 1999), 5.

The Dialogues of Plato, Benjamin Jowett, tr. (New York: Boni and Liveright, 1927), 162–63.

Gardner, John, *The Art of Fiction*. New York: Vintage, 1984.

Gutkind, Lee, *The Art of Creative Nonfiction* (New York: Wiley, 1997).

Hemingway, Ernest, "The Sea Change" in *The Short Stories of Ernest Hemingway* (New York: Scribner, 1964).

Hills, Rust, *Writing in General and the Short Story in Particular.*

Lamott, Anne, *Bird by Bird.*

McBride, James, *The Color of Water* (New York: Riverhead, 1996), 50–51.

Rainer, Tristine, *Your Life as Story.*

Scott, Alistair, "Coffee at the Café du Soleil," *Offshoots V, Writing from Geneva,* Geneva, 1991, 9–10.

Zinsser, William, *Inventing the Truth* (Boston: Houghton Mifflin, 1995).

LESSON SEVEN: TALES: FOLK, FAIRY, AND CONTEMPORARY

Barrett, Lynne, "Little Red Returns," *River City Magazine* (Memphis, TN), 2005.

Baugh, Susan, "Writing the Fairy Tale," workshop at International Women's Writing Guild Conference, Skidmore College, 2000.

Bettelheim, Bruno, *The Uses of Enchantment* (New York: Vintage, 1989).

Carter, Angela, *The Bloody Chamber* (New York: Penguin, 1979).

Chinen, Allan B., "The Six Statues" in *In the Ever After* (Chicago: Chiron, 1989), 95-96.

Estés, Clarissa Pinkola, *Women Who Run with the Wolves* (New York: Ballantine, 1995).

The Complete Grimms' Fairy Tales, Padraic Colum, introduction; Joseph Campbell, folkloristic commentary (New York: Pantheon, 1972), 319.

Grimms' Tales for Young and Old, Ralph Manheim, tr. (New York: Doubleday, 1977), 239–41.

Jung, C. G., "Mysterium Coniunctionis" (paragraph 706) in Edward F. Edinger, *The Mysterium Lectures* (Toronto: Inner City Books, 1995), 307-308.

Lewis, C.S., *The Lion, the Witch and the Wardrobe* (London: Penguin, 1962), 5.

Rainer, Tristine, *Your Life as Story* (New York: Tarcher/Putnam, 1998).

Stein, Murray and Lionel Corbett, eds., *Psyche's Stories* (Wilmette, IL: Chiron, 1991).

Von Franz, Marie-Louise, *Interpretation of Fairy Tales* (Boston: Shambhala, 1996).

————, *Shadow and Evil in Fairytales* (New York: Spring, 1986).

LESSON EIGHT: POETIC PROSE AND THE PROSE POEM

Barenblat, Rachel, *Prose Poems/Microfiction* (www.webdelsol.com/InPosse/barenblat.htm)

Benedikt, Michael, "Michael Benedikt Talks About Prose Poetry" (www.members.aol.com/benedit4)

Bly, Robert, "The Pine Cone" in *The Prose Poem, an International Journal,* Vol. 3, 1993. 16.

Boyd, Greg, "Lovers" in *Carnival Aptitude* (Santa Maria, CA: Asylum Arts Press, 1993).

Didion, Joan, *The Year of Magical Thinking* (London: Fourth Estate, 2005).

Forster, E.M., *Aspects of the Novel* (New York: Harvest, 1956).

Gardner, John, *The Art of Fiction.*

Hampl, Patricia, "Memory and Imagination" in *I Could Tell You Stories* (New

York: Norton, 1999), 21–22.

Hirshfield, Jane, *Nine Gates, Entering the Mind of Poetry* (New York: Harper-Collins, 1997).

Jenkins, Louis, "A Quiet Place" in *Nice Fish* (Duluth, MN: Holy Cow! Press, 1995).

Johnson, Peter, *The Prose Poem,* Vols. 1-10 (Providence, RI: Providence College, 1992–2000).

Pamuk, Orhan, *Snow* (London: Faber and Faber, 2004), 3-4.

Pinsky, Robert, *The Sounds of Poetry* (New York: Farrar, Straus and Giroux, 1998).

Shapiro, Myra, *I'll See You Thursday* (St. Paul, MN: Blue Sofa Press/Ally Press, 1996).

Tiberghien, Susan M., "Cinquefoil," *Circling to the Center* (New York: Paulist Press, 2000. 7).

Vreeland, Susan, *Girl in Hyacinth Blue* (New York: Penguin, 1999), 10, Reader Guide.

LESSON NINE: THE ALCHEMY OF IMAGINATION

Coelho, Paulo, *The Alchemist* (San Francisco: Harper San Francisco, 1995), 13–14, 153–54.

Dillard, Annie, *The Writing Life,* 3.

Hoffman, Eva, *Lost in Translation* (New York: Penguin, 1989), 5.

Jung, C. G., *Mysterium Coniunctionis* (Princeton, NJ: Princeton University Press, 1979).

Kidd, Sue Monk, *The Secret Life of Bees* (New York: Penguin, 2002).

Ondaatje, Michael, *Running in the Family,* 135.

Rilke, Rainer Maria, *Letters to a Young Poet,* 19.

The Secret of the Golden Flower, Richard Wilhelm, tr. (New York: Harcourt, 1962).

Tiberghien, Susan, "Pieces of Gold" in *Looking for Gold,* 153.

———, "Going Somewhere" (The Water Jug) in *Looking for Gold,* 18-19.

Von Franz, Marie-Louise, *Alchemy* (Toronto: Inner City Books, 1980).

Williams, Terry Tempest, *Red* (New York: Vintage, 2001), 160–61, 189.

LESSON TEN: MOSAICS AND MEMOIR

Armstrong, Karen, *The Spiral Staircase* (New York: Doubleday, 2005).

Atwood, Margaret, *Negotiating with the Dead* (New York: Cambridge University Press, 2002).

Augustine, Saint, *The Confessions* (New York: Vintage, 1998), 204, 214.

Auster, Paul, *The Invention of Solitude* (London: Faber and Faber, 1988), 29.

Didion, Joan, *The Year of Magical Thinking,* 3.

Dillard, Annie, *For the Time Being* (New York: Knopf, 1999).

———, "To Fashion a Text" in Zinsser, *Inventing the Truth,* 42–60.

Galeano, Eduardo, "The Fiesta" in *The Book of Embraces* (New York: Norton, 1992), 268.

———, interview in *Fourth Genre,* Fall 2001.

Garcia Marquez, Gabriel, *Living to Tell the Tale* (New York: Vintage, 2004), front page.

Gornick, Vivian, *The Situation and the Story* (New York: Farrar, Straus and Giroux, 2001).

Hampl, Patricia, "The Need to Say It" in Janet Sternburg, ed., *The Writer on Her Work,* Vol. 2 (New York: Norton, 1991).

Huggan, Isabel, *Belonging* (Toronto: Knopf Canada, 2003), 134–35.

McCourt, Frank, "The Memoir Explosion" in *Authors Guild Bulletin* (New York, Summer 1997), 30.

Merwin, W.S., *Summer Doorways* (New York: Shoemaker, Hoard, 2005).

Murdock, Maureen, *Unreliable Truth* (New York: Seal Press, 2003), 24–25.

Norris, Kathleen, *The Cloister Walk* (New York: Riverhead, 1996).

———, *Dakota.*

Ondaatje, Michael, *Running in the Family,* 21.

Prose, Francine, *Reading Like a Writer* (New York: HarperCollins, 2006), 3.

Rainer, Tristine, *Your Life as Story.*

Tiberghien, Susan, *Looking for Gold.*

————, *Circling to the Center.*

Walker, Alice, *The Way Forward Is with a Broken Heart* (New York: Random House, 2000), xiii.

Wiesel, Elie, *Night* (New York: Hill and Wang, 2006).

Wilde-Menozzi, Wallis, *Mother Tongue: An American Life in Italy* (New York: North Point, 1997), 332.

Talese, Gay, *Writer's Digest* interview, August, 2006. Cincinnati, OH: F+W Publications.

Zinsser, William, *Inventing the Truth.*

LESSON ELEVEN: REWRITING

Alvarez, Al, *Where Did It All Go Right?* (London: Richard Cohen Books, 1999), 3–4.

Cameron, Julia, *The Artist's Way.*

————, *The Right to Write.*

Carver, Raymond, "Rewriting" in George Plimpton, ed., *The Writer's Chapbook* (New York: Viking, 1989).

Gardner, John, *The Art of Fiction.*

Goldberg, Natalie, *Writing Down the Bones.*

Morrison, Toni, *Sula* (London: Triad-Grafton Books, 1986), 11.

O'Connor, Flannery, "Everything That Rises Must Converge" in *The Complete Stories* (New York: Farrar, Straus and Giroux, 1946), 405–421.

Plimpton, ed., *The Writer's Chapbook.*

Strand, Mark, quoted in "Improvisers and Revisers," *Poets & Writers,* May-June 2006.

Zinsser, William, *On Writing Well* (New York: Harper Perennial, 1990).

LESSON TWELVE: WRITING THE WAY HOME

Dillard, Annie, *The Writing Life,* 57.

Eire, Carlos, *Waiting for Snow in Havana* (New York: Free Press, 2003), 1–2.

Hamilton, Edith, *Mythology* (New York: Mentor, 1969).

Hammarskjöld, Dag, *Markings* (New York: Random House, 1983), 152.

Hillesum, Ettie, *An Interrupted Life,* 207–08.

Kerenyi, Karl, *The Gods of the Greeks* (London: Thames and Hudson), 1980

Homer, "Hymn to Hestia," *Homeric Hymns* 24.1, www.ancienthistory.about.com/
library/bl/bl_text_homerhymn_hestia

McDermott, Karen, "Three Pears," *Offshoots VII, Writing from Geneva,* Geneva,
2003, 10.

Rilke, Rainer Maria, *Letters to a Young Poet.*

Sarton, May, *Journal of a Solitude.*

Tiberghien, Susan, *Circling to the Center* (New York: Paulist Press, 2000).

———, "Maple Tree" in *Looking for Gold* (Einsiedeln, Switzerland: Daimon
Verlag, 1997), 54.

Wilde-Menozzi, Wallis, "The Oneness of Music" in Philip Zaleski, ed., *Best
Spiritual Writing* (San Francisco: HarperSanFrancisco, 2002), 248–58; first
appeared in *Agni Review,* # 53, New Jersey, 2001.

Williams, Terry Tempest, *Leap* (New York: Pantheon, 2000), 132.

General Bibliography by Author

Alvarez, Al. *Where Did It All Go Right?* London: Richard Cohen Books, 1999.

Armstrong, Karen. *The Spiral Staircase.* New York: Doubleday, 2005.

Atwan, Robert. *The Best American Essays 2001.* Boston: Houghton Mifflin, 2001.

Atwood, Margaret. *Negotiating with the Dead: A Writer on Writing.* New York: Cambridge University Press, 2002.

Augustine, Saint. *The Confessions.* New York: Vintage, 1998.

Auster, Paul. *The Invention of Solitude.* London: Faber and Faber, 1988.

Barrett, Lynne. "Little Red Returns." *River City Magazine,* 2005.

Bettelheim, Bruno. *The Uses of Enchantment: The Meaning and Importance of Fairy Tales.* New York: Vintage, 1989.

Bly, Robert. "The Pine Cone." *The Prose Poem: an International Journal,* Vol. 3, 1993.

Bosnak, Robert. *A Little Course in Dreams.* Boston: Shambhala, 1988.

Boyd, Greg. "The Lovers." *Carnival Aptitude: Being an Exuberance in Short Prose & Photomontage.* Santa Maria, CA: Asylum Arts Press, 1993.

Brande, Dorothea. *Becoming a Writer.* New York: Harcourt, Brace, 1934.

Cameron, Julia. *The Artist's Way.* New York: Tarcher/Putnam, 1992.

———. *The Right to Write.* New York: Tarcher/Putnam, 1999.

Capote, Truman. *In Cold Blood.* New York: Vintage International, 1991.

Carter, Angela. *The Bloody Chamber. New York: Penguin Books, 1979.*

Carver, Raymond. *"Rewriting." George Plimpton, ed., The Writers' Chapbook.* New York: Viking: 1989.

Chevalier, Tracey. *Girl with a Pearl Earring.* London: HarperCollins, 1999.

Chinen, Allan B. *In the Ever After.* Chicago: Chiron, 1989.

Clay, George. "When Everything Begins." *Fourth Genre,* East Lansing, MI: Michigan State University Press, Spring 2001.

Coelho, Paolo. *The Alchemist.* San Francisco: Harper SanFrancisco, 1995.

The Complete Grimms' Fairy Tales. Padraic Colum, introduction; Joseph Campbell, folkloristic commentary. New York: Pantheon, 1972.

The Dialogues of Plato. Benjamin Jowett, tr. New York: Boni & Liveright, 1927.

Didion, Joan. *The Year of Magical Thinking.* London: Fourth Estate, 2005.

Dillard, Annie. *For the Time Being.* New York: Knopf, 1999.

———. *The Writing Life.* New York: Harper & Row, 1989.

———. "To Fashion a Text" in Zinsser, William. *Inventing the Truth.* Boston: Houghton Mifflin, 1995.

Eire, Carlos. *Waiting for Snow in Havana.* New York: Free Press, 2003.

Elbow, Peter. *Writing with Power.* New York: Oxford University Press, 1981.

Epel, Naomi, ed. *Writers Dreaming.* New York: Vintage, 1994.

Estés, Clarissa Pinkola. *Women Who Run with the Wolves.* New York: Ballantine, 1995.

Forster, E.M. *Aspects of the Novel.* New York: Harcourt, 1956.

Galeano, Eduardo. *The Book of Embraces.* New York: Norton, 1992.

Garcia Marquez, Gabriel. *Living to Tell the Tale.* New York: Vintage, 2004.

Gardner, Janet E. "Gifts." *Vestal Review* 2005 (www.vestalreview.net/Gifts)

Gardner, John, *The Art of Fiction.* New York: Vintage, 1984.

Goldberg, Natalie. *Writing Down the Bones.* Boston: Shambala, 1986.

Gornick, Vivian. *The Situation and the Story.* New York: Farrar, Straus and Giroux, 2001.

Grimms' Tales for Young and Old: The Complete Stories. Ralph Manheim, tr. New York: Doubleday, 1977.

Guthrie, A.B. *A Field Guide to Writing Fiction.* New York: HarperCollins, 1991.

Gutkind, Lee. *The Art of Creative Nonfiction.* New York: Wiley, 1997.

Hamilton, Edith. *Mythology*. New York: Mentor, 1969.

Hammarskjöld, Dag. *Markings*. New York: Random House, 1983.

Hampl, Patricia. *I Could Tell You Stories: Sojourns in the Land of Memory*. New York: Norton, 1999.

———. "The Need to Say It" in Janet Sternburg, ed., *The Writer on Her Work*, Vol. 2 (New York: Norton) 1991.

Heilbrun, Carolyn. *Writing a Woman's Life*. New York: Ballantine, 1988.

Hemingway, Ernest. *The Short Stories of Ernest Hemingway*. New York: Scribner, 1964.

Hiestand, Emily, *The Very Rich Hours*, Boston: Beacon Press, 1992.

Illuminations of Hildegard of Bingen. Matthew Fox, commentary. Santa Fe: Bear & Company, 1985.

Hillesum, Ettie. *An Interrupted Life*. New York: Henry Holt, 1996.

Hills, Rust. *Writing in General and the Short Story in Particular*. Boston: Houghton Mifflin, 1987.

Hirshfield, Jane. *Nine Gates: Entering the Mind of Poetry*. New York: Harper-Collins, 1997.

Hoffman, Eva. *Lost in Translation*. New York: Penguin Books, 1989.

Holzer, Burghild Nina. *A Walk Between Heaven and Earth*. New York: Bell Tower, 1994.

Howe, Irving and Ilana Wiener Howe, eds. *Short Shorts*, London: Bantam, 1983.

Huggan, Isabel. *Belonging: A Home Away from Home*. Toronto: Knopf Canada, 2003.

Jenkins, Louis. *Nice Fish*. Duluth, MN: Holy Cow! Press, 1995.

Johnson, Peter, *The Prose Poem*, Vols. 1–10. Providence, RI: Providence College, 1992–2000.

Joyce, James, *Dubliners*. London: Penguin, 2000.

Jung, C. G. *Civilization in Transition*, second ed. Princeton: Princeton University Press, 1970.

———. *Mysterium Coniunctionis*. Princeton, NJ: Princeton University Press, 1979.

————. *Memories, Dreams, Reflections*. London: Fontana Paperbacks, 1989.

Kerenyi, Karl. *The Gods of the Greeks*. London: Thames and Hudson, 1980.

Kidd, Sue Monk. *The Secret Life of Bees*. New York: Penguin, 2002.

King, Stephen. *On Writing*. New York: Scribner, 2000.

Kingsolver, Barbara. *Small Wonder*. London: Faber & Faber, 2002.

Lamott, Anne. *Bird by Bird*. New York: Doubleday, 1995.

Lemack, Carie. "9/11 means heroism—and division." *International Herald Tribune,* September 10–11, 2005.

Lewis, C.S. *The Lion, the Witch and the Wardrobe*. London: Penguin Books, 1962.

Lopate, Phillip. *The Art of the Personal Essay: An Anthology from the Classical Era to the Present*. New York: Doubleday, 1994.

Lott, Bret. "Genesis," *Creative Nonfiction* #27, 2005.

Marquez, Gabriel, *Living to Tell the Tale,* New York: Vintage, 2004

McBride, James. *The Color of Water*. New York: Riverhead, 1996.

McCauley, Lucy, Amy C. Carlson, and Jennifer Leo, eds. *A Woman's Path: Women's Best Spiritual Travel Writing*. Berkeley, CA: Travelers' Tales, 2000.

McDermott, Karen. "Three Pears." *Offshoots VII, Writing from Geneva,* Geneva, 2003.

Merwin, W.S. *Summer Doorways*. New York: Shoemaker, Hoard, 2005.

Morrison, Toni. *Sula*. London: Triad-Grafton Books, 1986.

Murdock, Maureen. *Unreliable Truth: On Memoir and Memory*. New York: Seal Press, 2003.

Norris, Kathleen. *The Cloister Walk*. New York: Riverhead, 1996.

————. *Dakota: A Spiritual Geography*. Boston: Houghton Mifflin, 1993.

O'Connor, Flannery, *The Complete Stories* (New York: Farrar, Straus and Giroux, 1946.

————. *Mystery and Manners*. New York: Farrar, Straus and Giroux, 1984.

Ondaatje, Michael. *Running in the Family*. London: Picador, 1984.

Paley, Grace, *The Collected Stories,* New York: Farrar, Straus and Giroux, 1994.

Pamuk, Orhan. *Snow*. London: Faber and Faber, 2004.

Pinsky, Robert. *The Sounds of Poetry*. New York: Farrar, Straus and Giroux, 1998.

Plimpton, George. *The Writer's Chapbook*. New York: Viking, 1989.

Prose, Francine. *Reading Like a Writer*. New York: HarperCollins, 2006.

Rainer, Tristine. *Your Life as Story*. New York: Tarcher/Putnam, 1998.

Rilke, Rainer Maria. *Letters to a Young Poet*. New York: Norton, 1962.

Sarton, May. *Journal of a Solitude*. New York: Norton, 1973.

Scarfe, Eunice. "When My Mourning Comes." Banff: Alberta, 2002.

Schiwy, Marlene. *A Voice of Her Own*. New York: Simon and Schuster, 1996.

Scott, Alistair. "Coffee at the Café du Soleil." *Offshoots V, Writing from Geneva*. Geneva, 1991.

Shapiro, Myra. *I'll See You Thursday*. St. Paul, MN: Blue Sofa Press/Ally Press, 1996.

Stein, Murray and Lionel Corbett, eds. *Psyche's Stories: Modern Jungian Interpretations of Fairy Tales*. Wilmette, IL: Chiron, 1991.

Sternburg, Janet, ed. *The Writer on Her Work*, Vol. 1. New York: Norton, 1980.

———. *The Writer on Her Work*, Vol. 2. New York: Norton, 1991.

Stevens, Sidney, "When Times Were Tough," "My Turn" essay, *Newsweek*, July 28, 2003.

Strand, Mark, quoted in "Improvisers and Revisers," *Poets & Writers*, May-June 2006.

Tiberghien, Susan. *Circling to the Center: One Woman's Encounter with Silent Prayer*. New York: Paulist Press, 2000.

———. *Footsteps: A European Album*. Philadelphia: Xlibris, 2005.

———. *Looking for Gold: A Year in Jungian Analysis*. Einsiedeln, Switzerland: Daimon Verlag, 1997.

Udall, Brady. "The Wig." *Story*, Cincinnati, OH: F & W Publications, 1994.

Ueland, Brenda. *If You Want to Write*. St. Paul, MN: Graywolf Press, 1987.

Van de Castle, Robert. *Our Dreaming Mind*. New York: Ballantine, 1994.

Vivian, Robert, "Light Calling to Other Light," *Fourth Genre,* Michigan State University, Spring 2000.

Von Franz, Marie-Louise. *Alchemy.* Toronto: Inner City Books, 1980.

———. *Interpretation of Fairy Tales.* Boston: Shambhala, 1996.

———. *Shadow and Evil in Fairytales.* New York: Spring Publications, 1986.

Vreeland, Susan. *Girl in Hyacinth Blue.* New York: Penguin Books, 1999.

Walker, Alice. *Living by the Word.* New York: Harcourt, 1988.

———. *The Way Forward Is with a Broken Heart,* New York: Random House, 2000.

Wiesel, Elie. *Night.* New York: Hill and Wang, 2006.

Wilde-Menozzi, Wallis. "The Oneness of Music" in Philip Zaleski, ed., *Best Spiritual Writing* (San Francisco: HarperSanFrancisco, 2002).

———. *Mother Tongue: An American Life in Italy.* New York: North Point, 1997.

Williams, Terry Tempest. *Leap.* New York: Pantheon, 2000.

———, *Red: Passion and Patience in the Desert.* New York: Vintage, 2001.

Wilson, Kevin. "Carried Away." *Quick Fiction,* Issue Four, Jamaica Plain, MA, 2003.

Woodman, Marion. *Bone: Dying to Life.* New York: Viking, 2000.

Zaleski, Philip, ed. *Best Spiritual Writing.* San Francisco: HarperSanFrancisco, 2003.

Zinsser, William. *Inventing the Truth.* Boston: Houghton Mifflin, 1995.

———. *On Writing Well,* fourth ed. New York: Harper Perennial, 1990.

Bibliography of Selected Anthologies and Reviews

Atwan, Robert, ed. Best *American Essays* (annual). Boston: Houghton Mifflin.

Howe, Irving and Ilana Wiener Howe, eds. *Short Shorts*. London: Bantam, 1983.

Kenison, Katrina, editor. *Best American Short Stories* (annual). Boston: Houghton Mifflin.

Moffett, James, ed. *Points of Departure: An Anthology of Nonfiction*. New York: Mentor, 1985.

Shepard, Robert and James Thomas, eds. *Sudden Fiction Continued: 60 New Short-Short Stories*. New York: Norton, 1996.

————. *Sudden Fiction International: 60 Short-Short Stories*. New York: Norton, 1989.

————. *New Sudden Fiction*. New York: Norton, 2007.

Thomas, James, Denise Thomas, Tom Hazuka, eds. *Flash Fiction, 72 Very Short Stories*. New York: Norton, 1992.

Wilson, Jason, ed. *Best American Travel Writing* (annual). Boston: Houghton Mifflin.

Zaleski, Philip, ed. *Best Spiritual Writing*. San Francisco: HarperSanFrancisco.

Creative Nonfiction, #27, Pittsburgh, Creative Nonfiction Foundation.

Christian Science Monitor, Boston.

Fourth Genre, Michigan State University Press.

International Herald Tribune, Paris.

Newsweek, "My Turn" essays, New York.

New York Times Magazine, "My Life" Essays, New York.

Poets & Writers Magazine, New York (www.pw.org/mag).

Offshoots, Writing from Geneva (biennial), Geneva Writers Group.

Quick Fiction, Jamaica Plain, MA.

The Prose Poem, Vol. 1–9, Peter Johnson, Providence, RI: Providence College.

Travelers' Tales, Larry Habegger and James O'Reilly, eds., Palo Alto, CA.

Vestal Review, 2005 (www.vestalreview.net)

The Writer, Boston. (www.writermag.com)

Writer's Digest, Cincinnati, OH. (www.writersdigest.com)

CREDITS

From *Where Did It All Go Right*, by Al Alvarez, copyright © 1999 by Al Alvarez, Bloomsbury

From *The Confessions*, by Saint Augustine, Random House

From *The Invention of Solitude*, by Paul Auster, copyright © Paul Auster 1982. Used by permission of Faber and Faber Ltd. Reprinted with permission of the Carol Mann Agency.

"Little Red Returns" from *River City Magazine*, copyright © Lynne Barrett, with permission of Lynne Barrett.

"The Pine Cone" from *The Prose Poem*, copyright © Robert Bly, with permission of Robert Bly.

"Lovers" from *Carnival Aptitude*, copyright © Greg Boyd, 1993, used by permission of Leaping Dog Press/Asylum Arts Press.

From *Girl with a Pearl Earring*, by Tracey Chevalier, copyright © 1999 by Tracey Chevalier 1999. Used by permission of Plume, an imprint of Penguin Group (USA) Inc. By permission of HarperCollins Publishers Ltd.

"The Six Statues," from *In the Ever After*, Allan B. Chinen, Chiron Publications, with permission of Lantern Books, New York.

"Where Everything Begins," by George R. Clay. This work originally appeared in *Fourth Genre*, Vol. No.3:1, 2001 published by Michigan State University Press.

From *The Alchemist*, by Paulo Coelho, English translation copyright © by Paulo Coelho and Alan R. Clarke. Reprinted by permission of HarperCollins Publishers Ltd, copyright © 1988 Paolo Coehlo.

From the Introduction, Annie Dillard, in *Best American Essays* 1988, Houghton Mifflin

From *Waiting for Snow in Havana: Confessions of a Cuban Boy*, by Carlos Eire. Copyright © 2003 by Carlos Eire. Reprinted with permission of The Free Press, a Division of Simon & Schuster Adult Publishing Group. All rights reserved.

From *Writers Dreaming*, by Naomi Epel, Crown edition, with permission of Random House, Inc.

Index